Valiant Heart Trilogy

Book 1: The Call to Arms
Book 2: Blood and Fire
Book 3: Airship of Dreams

THE CALL TO ARMS

C.M.S. Thornton

Copyright © C.M.S. Thornton 2024

The right of C.M.S. Thornton to be identified as author of this work has been asserted by her in accordance with the Copyright, Designs and Patents Act, 1988.

All rights reserved. No part of this book may be reproduced or transmitted by any person or entity (including Google, Amazon or similar organisations) in any form or by any means, electronic or mechanical, including photocopying, recording or by any information storage and retrieval system, without prior permission in writing from the publisher.

A catalogue record for this book is available from the National Library of Australia.

Author: Thornton, C.M.S., author.
Title: The call to arms : the clerk who dared the great adventure / C.M.S. Thornton.
ISBN: 9781923212022 (hardcover)
ISBN: 9781923212039 (paperback)

Series: Thornton, C.M.S. Valiant heart ; 2.
Notes: Includes bibliographical references.
Subjects: Biography--Non fiction.
Genre: Non fiction.
Cover image includes Norman Lindsay's "The Trumpet Calls", Alamy ID:M7FHWB

www.leavesofgoldpress.com
ABN 67 099 575 078

THE CALL TO ARMS

The Clerk Who Dared the Great Adventure

Squadron Leader William Palstra M.C., B.A.

1891 - 1930

First World War soldier and airman

~ Salvation Army ~

~ 39th Battalion, Australian Imperial Force ~

~ Australian Flying Corps ~

~ University of Melbourne ~

~ Royal Australian Air Force ~

'Nobody would have guessed—least of all himself—
that beneath the waistcoat of this humble office clerk
there beat the heart of a leader of men
and a conqueror of the skies . . .'

This book is dedicated to the families of the Australians and New Zealanders
who took part in the Great War 1914-1918;
also to the Palstras, the Holdaways,
and my sisters.

W & K London. R101 THE WORLD'S LARGEST AIRSHIP No 199.
OVER LONDON.

CONTENTS

Introduction..xi

Prologue..xiii

Palstra Family Tree...7

Part I 1915: A Victorian Clerk

    1: Melbourne in 1914...9

    2: The Outbreak of the Great War................................21

    3: The Anzacs...33

    4: Family Life...39

Part II 1915: The Bugles of England

    1: The Hero's Return..43

    2: The Call to Arms...49

Part III 1916: To Arms! is the Call

    1: Enlistment...57

    2: Ballarat Training Camp..65

Part IV 1916: Where Are Our Uniforms?

    1: A Temporary Corporal 71

    2: A Decision is Made 79

Part V 1916: Dash and Determination

    1: Preparing to Depart 83

    2: Marching Through the City 91

    3: Embarkation 107

Part VI 1916: Voyage Across the World

    1 : The Voyage Begins. 127

    2: Shipboard Life. 141

    3: Cape Town 145

Part VII 1916: To England's Shores

    1 Crossing the Equator 155

    2: The Cape Verde Islands and Beyond 163

    3: Arrival in England 169

Part VIII 1916: On Salisbury Plain

    1: The Plain 173

    2: Aeroplanes over Stonehenge 185

Part IX 1916/17: City of Dreaming Spires

    1: Oxford. 213

Part X 1917: Across the Straits of Dover

    1: The Guns Thundered All Night Long. 227

Bibliography 235

INTRODUCTION

The house of my childhood was haunted.

History permeated our family life, for it had soaked into the very fabric of the walls. It seeped from the antiques and curios brought back by our globe-trotting ancestors—the Chinese and Dutch ornaments, and the Māori artefacts. The past lurked, too, in the photograph albums, the wooden aeroplane propeller in the hall cupboard, the shoe-boxes filled with slightly tarnished AIF 'rising sun' buttons and badges, the handful of shrapnel, the old upright piano, the derelict chicken coop at the bottom of the garden, the old wooden sea-trunk in my bedroom, plastered all over with faded P&O steamship luggage labels that hinted at long-ago journeys to exotic places...

Ghosts, nameless and silent, were central to that history, emanating from memories that were not our own. Throughout the years, as my sisters and I grew up, these wraiths walked among us, pervading the waking hours and dreams of the adults. With every solemn tick of the vintage clock on the mantelpiece, they gradually increased their power over us, too.

The adults were unable to escape the influence of the past, let alone shield the children. There was nothing deliberate on their part; they did not intend to transmit the hauntings that bled into our young bones, but it happened. They were not conscious of it, and nor were we. There was no name for this phenomenon then, but there is now: 'Inter-generational trauma'.

We children did not yet understand it, but one 'present absence' in particular was the focus of unspeakable, long-buried anguish and longing. His legacy continues to affect our family to this day, almost a hundred years after his death.

A massive bureau, or chest-of-drawers, stood in the hallway of my childhood home. Made of age-darkened mahogany, it contained a hidden compartment; a long, low, deep drawer with no handles, which appeared, to the uninitiated, to be part of the decoration. Only those who were aware of its existence knew the trick of opening it. Within that drawer, known only to members of the immediate family, a multitude of old letters and diaries lay concealed for decades.

These faithfully preserved letters and diaries were written by, and to, my mother's father. For it was he whose terrible absence was the vortex into which the threads of our young lives were being drawn, and the burden we were destined to bear.

For as long as I can remember, an irresistible need to do the impossible, to bring him back to life, has ridden on the shoulders of me and my loved ones, like some demon. We each coped in our own way.

When I reached adulthood, my way of coping was to use the letters and diaries concealed in that hidden drawer to tell his story. I was also able to include many of the intriguing sepia photos from the well-preserved family albums.

Inter-generational trauma drove me to document his life almost day-by-day, extrapolating to fill the gaps in the first-hand material. This gave me around 632,000 words. Having condensed them (which was incredibly difficult), I have finally completed the duty that seemed to be laid upon me at birth. In the only way possible have (I hope), after decades of work and longing, immortalised my grandfather, William Palstra.

C.M.S. Thornton

PROLOGUE

Every event has consequences. Those consequences can ripple far across the universe, far into the future. In truth, they never really fade, even when we are no longer aware of them. After the primal event has passed out of human knowledge, still the effects flow inexorably on.

When His Majesty's airship R.101 fell out of the sky in 1930, her terrible ending seemed to herald the fading of the most far-reaching empire the world has ever known. It caused other effects, too—powerful enough to impact the lives of generations. Effects that, to this day, continue to reverberate through time and space . . .

On the evening of October 4th, 1930, rain-clouds were piling up in the skies over Bedfordshire, England.

At the Cardington Air Base, the British Empire's new airship, the largest object ever to fly, hovered two hundred feet above the ground, looking like some surreal deep-sea fish. She was tethered by the nose to the top of her mooring mast. A dazzling beam from a flood-lamp pierced the gathering dusk. Against the darkening skies, the massive hull of the cigar-shaped dirigible shimmered silver-grey. She floated parallel to the fields below, where a large crowd milled about, their faces upturned, marvelling at the sight. Surely this this improbable machine was too huge, too cumbersome to be suspended magically in the air, trembling slightly in the breeze, like a leaf!

The R101 being hauled to her mooring mast

With a length of 237 m (777 ft) the R.101 airship was longer than three Boeing 747s. That is more than twice the length of an international soccer pitch, or 2 ½ times the length of an American football field.

Though built to float, she weighed approximately one hundred and eighty tons; far more when fully loaded. Her motors, carried in five egg-shaped gondolas supported beneath the hull, were compression ignition engines developing five hundred and eighty-five horsepower each, and burning heavy oil. The R.101 was indeed a spectacular sight; a leviathan looming against the rain-clouds like some flying monster from an alien world.

Thousands of spectators lined the roads bordering the Air Base, whose gates were closed to the general public. Rows of parked motor-cars, head-lamps blazing, helped to illuminate the scene.

The R101 at Cardington mooring mast

At 7.36 p.m. the great airship cast off from her mooring mast and began to rise.

'Hurrah! Hurrah!' chorused the spectators. 'God speed! Good luck!'

To the roar of enthusiastic cheering from the cap-waving crowd below, she slowly gained height, buoyed by the five million cubic feet of hydrogen gas sealed within her envelope. The crew of the airship evidently heard the cheering, and responded by flashing their lamps.

This was the beginning of the R.101's first international voyage, and she was bound for India. Her first stop was to be Ismailia, on the Suez Canal in Egypt, for re-fuelling. The 54 men on board—48 crew members and six passengers—were preparing to enjoy a long, comfortable flight.

On completion, the R.101 boasted luxurious passenger accommodation and service to rival that of the greatest ocean liners. Her sumptuous outfitting could be compared to the ship *RMS Titanic*. Potted palms and Axminster carpet adorned the elegant dining room. The dinner service had been specially commissioned, and bore her insignia. The airship officers wore dark blue uniforms. Their caps bore the blue and gold badge embroidered with 'Airship R.101', topped by a crown representing King George V.

Dining room of the R101 with the chief steward, Albert Savidge.

PASSENGERS IN THE LOUNGE ROOM OF THE R101

The R.101 was to be among the first of a fleet of commercial dirigibles, 'liners of the skies', capable of carrying huge numbers of passengers back and forth across the globe.

The huge volumes of hydrogen gas carried in bags inside the airship's envelope made her lighter than air. It also made her highly flammable. Passengers and crew had to wear shoes without nails in the soles, lest the steel strike sparks. Smoking was forbidden, except in the specially fire-proofed 'smoking room'.

The R.101 had been carefully trimmed before leaving the mast. As she slipped her mooring cable she gave a slight lurch—watchers recalled that she dipped sharply—so Captain Irwin ordered four tons of water ballast to be dropped at once from the bows and amidships, in order to gain height. A warning from the meteorological office had told him to expect winds of up to forty to fifty miles per hour, worse than any conditions a British airship had experienced over land in the past.

The airship swung easily clear on an almost level keel, and very slowly wheeled away to gain height. Moving steadily south, she sent out regular radio messages so that her course could be followed. She circled around the nearby town of Bedford before rising to a thousand feet, then to fifteen hundred feet as she moved towards London.

Soon after she left Cardington, rain began to fall.

The R101 in flight

As the R.101 passed across England heading for the coast, householders peered out of their upper storey windows, eager to see the famous dirigible they had read about in the newspapers. They could see her huge bulk passing by, above the tree-tops. Her lights illuminated the surrounding landscape, glinting on silver spears of rain that stabbed through the darkness. Had the householders been able to look through the airship's windows into the interior, they might have glimpsed the passengers and officers gathered on the promenade deck, enjoying the view of the ground below.

The experienced crew on board expressed no concerns about the airship's performance in their wireless messages. At 9.21 p.m. the airship reported, 'Over London, All well. Moderate rain . . . course now set for Paris.' The message also gave the wind speed as 25 miles an hour—less than anticipated.

Being so heavily laden with passengers, luggage, fuel and water ballast, the airship continued to gain altitude slowly. She was still flying quite low when she passed over London, and her own radioed description of her manoeuvre before crossing the hills to the south was, 'Gradually increasing height so as to avoid high land'.

Near Hastings she left the English coast.

So vast was her envelope that a film of water only one sixty-fourth of an inch thick (0.4 mm) on the fabric would add eight tons to her weight. It was raining hard over the English Channel and, burdened beneath the weight of the downpour, the great silver dirigible fought her way with some difficulty, a thirty-five mile an hour sou-wester hammering on her starboard beam.

As she passed over the sea, a moderately serious engine problem occurred. The winds picked up and she slowly lost height until she reached the alarmingly low altitude of about seven hundred and fifty feet. Those on board could see the white caps of the foaming waves below.

At 10 p.m., the height coxswain, whose sole responsibility was maintaining correct altitude, received a visit from the first officer, Lieutenant Commander Atherstone. The more experienced airship pilot took over the wheel himself for a while until he had managed to achieve a considerable increase in altitude. Then he handed back the controls to the coxswain, warning him not to let the R.101 go below a thousand feet again.

By the time the R.101 had reached the French coast the engineers had corrected the mechanical problem. She made France over the Point de St Quentin and set a course direct for Paris. Strong winds were pummelling her vast envelope, and rain poured down in torrents.

At midnight, the airship sent out a further message. In spite of the rough weather conditions and serious trouble in maintaining height, its words betrayed no real fears on the part of the airship's guests and crew—

> After an excellent supper our distinguished passengers smoked a final cigar and having sighted the French coast have now gone to bed to rest after the excitement of their leavetaking.
>
> All essential services are functioning satisfactorily. The crew have settled down to watch-keeping routine.

R.101 sent out a regular position report at 1.28 am. At 1.30 she passed over the village of Saint-Valery-sur-Somme, appearing so low that the inhabitants scrambled from their beds, certain she would scrape the rooves off their houses. Slowly the airship thundered away into the pitch-dark night.

She sent another routine wireless transmission at 1.51, by which time she was approaching Beauvais, north of Paris. As she passed slightly to the east of the town, the roar of her engines awoke the townsfolk and frightened the children. People rushed to the windows to catch a glimpse of this historic sight; the majestic dirigible flying over their heads with her red and green warning lights twinkling, buffeted by rain and storm clouds.

After 2.07 a.m. there were no more messages from the R.101. Just outside Beauvais, with no warning at all, she went into a steep dive. She tilted so sharply that the engineers manning the ship were thrown off balance, and furniture shot forward across the decks. The height coxswain pulled hard on his wheel in an effort to right the airship, and managed to get her on an even keel once more. Within seconds, however, she plunged down again and this time the cox could do nothing to pull her out of the dive.

The officers in command could see what was coming. They ordered all engines to be cut dead—although in the confusion only one was stopped—and warning bells were rung throughout the airship.

It is difficult to imagine, but there was no panic. Airship flight is normally so smooth and buoyant, and altitude changes so much a part of the pattern, that few people would leap to the idea of 'crashing' in the way that modern aircraft passengers might. The professional men on board were trained to remain calm in dangerous situations; besides, it was just not 'the thing' to panic in front of one's peers. Perhaps also their faith in God and the British Air Ministry held firm.

The chief coxswain had time to go aft, where the crew members were sleeping, to announce quite matter-of-factly, 'We're down, lads.'

With a great grinding noise of engines ceasing and metal grating on metal, the airship lumbered to the earth and slid several yards along the ground.

Then, less than a minute after her last wireless transmission, she exploded into flames. A crashing roar swept through the valley as five million cubic feet of hydrogen ignited.

It shook the nearby village of Allonne to its foundations, and shattered windows. Sheets of flame towered into the sky. The furnace that was once an airship lit up the countryside with a ghastly yellow light, like some nightmarish sun. Night had turned into day.

People in the vicinity of Beauvais were awakened by the thunder. On rushing to their windows, they saw streaks of light soaring across the sky.

Next day, all that could be seen was a massive tangle of scorched metal. The twisted, burnt and charred framework was all that remained of the glorious R.101. She had been completely destroyed by fire. Forty-eight men perished out of a total of fifty-four passengers and crew.

That tragedy finished the British airship industry and was counted among the worst disasters of the twentieth century.

One of those aboard was Squadron Leader William Palstra, M.C., B.A.

This is his story.

PALSTRA FAMILY TREE

Wiebe PALSTRA (b. 4 March 1867 Harlingen, Friesland, Netherlands d. 1944) married **Jacoba Christina Hendrika ENGELBERT VAN BEVERVOORDE** (b. 29 December 1858 Deventer, or Hasselt, Overijssel, Netherlands. d. 1935). Their children:

- William (b. 8 October 1891 Zwolle, Overijssel, Netherlands. d. 5 October 1930, France)
- Henrietta Christina Alberdina (b. 10 October 1892 Amsterdam, Netherlands. d. 23 July 1969 USA?)
- Charles Engelbert (13 January 1893? 94? Amsterdam, Netherlands. d. Australia) Probably born in 1893.
- Frank Elwyn (b. 5 October 1896 St. Jean, Belgium. d. 23 September 1957, Australia)
- Blanche Evangeline (b. 14 October 1898 Brussels, Belgium. d. November 1978 Melbourne, Australia)
- James Victor (b. 26 October 1900 Belgium.)
- John Bernard Philip (b. 7 September 1904 Johannesburg, South Africa. death date unknown, possibly September 24 1957 Australia)

William Palstra when young (possibly a teenager)

'Only time, not space, separates us from the past.'

~ Author unknown ~

Part 1
1915: A Victorian Clerk[1]

1915: A Victorian Clerk | 1: Melbourne in 1914

The rattle of carriage wheels, the clip-clop of horses' hoofs on pavement, the roar of a bus or motor car, a sudden shout rising above the city's hum, the shrill, silver clang! of a cable-tram's bell; these sounds drift through the narrow, dusty panes of the office windows overlooking Collins Street, Melbourne, in September 1915.

At number 252, the home of the Pianola Company, twenty-four-year-old William Palstra works as a company clerk. His desk is on the first floor above the shop, beneath the window overlooking the street. Picture this lean, clean-shaven young man clad in plain trousers and matching waistcoat—grey or dark brown in colour—with a tie neatly knotted about his neck. From his waistcoat pocket peeps the patent Sheaffer fountain-pen filler he had brought with him when he first set foot in Australia, twelve months earlier. His jacket and Fedora hat dangle from a hook by the door. The jacket, being old and much-worn, shows signs of wear at the elbows.

---

1   Australians pronounced 'clerk' the Britsh way, as 'clark,' until the late 20th century.

The young man's short, light brown hair falls across his pale forehead. His shirtsleeves are rolled up to the elbow to save the cuffs from becoming stained with ink. A typewriter—most likely a Remington—squats on the desk in front of him. The Pianola Company's ornate letterhead stands up from between its rollers, followed by paragraphs of correspondence to which Will is adding, tapping rapidly and fluently on the keys, a slight frown of concentration furrowing his brow.

'Ting!' chimes the Remington. With practised ease, Will flicks the lever. The carriage slides smoothly to the right, and he begins typing a new line.

From the shop downstairs, loud and tuneful notes waft to the ears of Will and his co-workers. The Pianola Company sells instruments known as player pianos, or autopianos.

During the early 20th century, gramophones existed, but their sound reproduction was poor. Many people could play musical instruments, but those who did not possess that skill had to go to church to hear music—or music-halls, concerts, public ceremonies or bandstands in public parks, or parties at the home of musician friends. Alternatively, they could hope to thrill to the loud music of The Salvation Army's gleaming brass bands oomp-pahing through the streets of the city and suburbs.

If you wanted to hear good music in your own home on a regular basis, but couldn't play an instrument yourself, pianolas were your best option (assuming you could afford one!). You only had to sit down at the keyboard, and work the foot-pedals at the base of the piano. The loud and accurate melodies of pianolas were a real asset for parties, because guests could gather around the instrument for a singalong. All the popular songs could be purchased on paper rolls that fitted in the body of the instrument, and they came with printed booklets of lyrics. When pianolas began to be mass produced, their popularity in wealthier households grew rapidly.

It's likely that Will quite enjoyed working for the Pianola Company. An accomplished cornet and mandolin player himself, he relished music. The piano melodies drifting from the downstairs showroom must have made a pleasant change from the racket he was making on his typewriter.

Across the nation pianolas were currently thumping out popular songs such as 'Act Your Part, Australia'. After war was declared in 1914, Australian composers had rushed to produce new, patriotic songs like this:

'Comes the message from afar

You and we one people are

Help us in a righteous war,

Children of Australia!

'Let your soldiers brave and bold

From the land of wattle-gold

Britain's glorious arms uphold

Rally up Australia! [2]*'*

Will had lived in six different countries. Born in the Netherlands, he spent his childhood and youth with his family in France, Belgium and South Africa before moving to England and then Australia. His parents spoke Dutch and English, while people around him spoke French, Flemish, German, English and Afrikaans.

English was the language the Palstra family used amongst themselves. Like all Australians during that era, they identified themselves as citizens of the British Empire. Will had recently spent a couple of years living in London, and when he spoke, his accent would have sounded—to Australian ears—distinctly English as he bade a cordial 'Cheerio!' to his fellow workers at noon on that Saturday.

---

[2] 'Act Your Part, Australia'. Words by H. Tremlett Hull, music by Florence Hull.

Imagine Will stepping out the front door of the Pianola Company's premises on that Saturday afternoon, at the close of working-hours. It is Melbourne through which he strides this day; the country's capital; the financial centre of Australia and New Zealand, the largest city in Australia and the second largest in the British Empire. During the 1880s it had been the richest city in the world. Built on the gold rush, bustling, stately, fashionable, thriving, modern, Melbourne was one of Earth's great metropolises, and it is Will's new home.

At this hour on a Saturday, when the Pianola Company is closing its doors for the weekend, the afternoon is getting into full swing. The footpaths are crowded with people, young and old—on their way home from work, heading for the pub, patronising the coffee-houses or making their way to the Melbourne Cricket Ground to watch the 1915 VFL football Preliminary Final.

Other Melbournians are simply 'doing the Block'—strolling, congregating and promenading up and down in the heart of the city. Altogether, it is a pleasant and lively scene.

Sepia photographs from 1915 show the people crowding Melbourne's pavements—clerks, lawyers, merchants from the Port of Melbourne and other businessmen dressed, like Will, in three piece suits and fedora hats; children in sailor suits trotting along, towed by mothers and aunts in long skirts; labourers sporting cloth caps and trousers held up with braces; fashionable ladies in lacy shirtwaists and large, feathered hats.

Soldiers can be glimpsed among the throng; young men on leave from their training camps, striding along in their khaki-coloured uniforms and slouch hats, their Australian Imperial Force (AIF) badges glinting in the spring sunshine.

Carriages and motor vehicles bowl up and down the wide road, mingling with all manner of vehicles—steam buses, trams, bicycles, Hansom cabs, and horse-drawn delivery carts whose proprietors' names are painted in large letters on the sides. Cyclists weave in and out of the traffic. Street-wise dogs trot purposefully across the carriageway.

A few private motor cars with shiny, bulbous headlamps are parked at the kerbsides. The drivers of these new-fangled motor cars direct them exactly as they had directed their old horse-drawn carriages. If they wish to turn around and go in the opposite direction they merely wait for a break in the traffic and do so. If they wish to overtake a slower vehicle they merely swerve around it. Automated traffic signal systems have yet to be invented. It is not uncommon for motor car drivers to speed recklessly along the thoroughfare, endangering everyone in their path.

At times, as many pedestrians appear to be crossing the road as are walking along the footpath. Any citizen wanting to get from one side to the other chooses a moment to risk dodging between cyclists and horse-drawn cabs, motor cars and overcrowded cable-trams; not to mention the odd pile of horse manure. The city of Melbourne employed far fewer traffic policemen than Will had seen in the narrow and overcrowded streets of London.

Imagine the scene:

At the news-stands near the imposing façade of the Queen Victoria Buildings, newspaper boys are calling out the day's headlines: 'Read all about it!' Copies of *The Age* and *The Argus* lie stacked next to the illustrated ladies' magazines. With a shiny penny so newly minted that the moulded head of King George V seems to be leaping out of the bronze, Will buys the afternoon edition of *The Age* and tucks the rolled-up newspaper under his arm. Along the wide avenue of Swanston Street, stately Victorian edifices tower three to four stories high. Will strikes out purposefully, eager to be on time for his train.

A spectacular view of Flinders Street Station opens out as he rounds the corner of 'Young and Jackson's Princes Bridge Hotel'. Across the busy intersection the red brick and golden cream stucco of the grand baroque railway terminus, completed only five years earlier, gleams in the sunlight. Above the arched entrance with its nine clocks, the magnificent copper domes and soaring clock tower glimmer like the roofs of some fabled palace in far-off India.

The young clerk crosses the intersection, heading not for Flinders Street Station but for its sister station, Prince's Bridge, on the opposite corner. Dodging between pedestrians and trams, he hurries past the stall selling fruit and cigarettes. After passing through the turnstiles, he descends the slope leading down to the platform that serves the Epping Line, where a small crowd is waiting for the next train.

Running to schedule, the train arrives enveloped in clouds of hissing steam, puffing and chuffing, smoke pouring from the locomotive's stack. When all passengers have climbed in, the uniformed station master peers up and down the platform to check that no one is still getting on or off. A guard leans out of the last carriage. The station master yells 'All aboard!', then blows his whistle and waves a flag, whereupon the guard flourishes his own flag, the locomotive's whistle screeches and the train slowly moves off.

Will sits in the gently rocking carriage reading his newspaper, barely aware of the syncopated clattering of wheels on tracks, while the city buildings roll out of sight and the leafy streets of the suburbs begin sliding into view. The scene is very different from his life in London, when he had worked for The Salvation Army.

To understand the Palstra family, it is necessary to know something of the history of The Salvation Army.

The Army's beginnings date back to 1865 in England, when William Booth preached the gospel to the poor and underprivileged. By 1867 he had founded a ministry known as The Christian Mission, which offered basic schooling, reading rooms, penny banks, soup kitchens, and relief aid to the destitute. Booth's wife, Catherine, established equality for women. They could be ordained ministers of the gospel, and hold leadership positions within the organisation.

In 1878 Booth changed the name of his ministry to The Salvation Army and the organisation's now-familiar trappings began to appear, including their military-style uniform. Military terms became standard. The full-time ordained ministers and staff of the organisation were known as Officers, and they adopted military rank titles according to seniority. The part-time, ordinary members were called Soldiers. William Booth became The Salvation Army's General. The Mission-Stations (Churches) were henceforth entitled Corps. Flags, badges and brass bands were added.

The Army offered spiritual counsel, a sense of community and practical support to people around the world, regardless of race, creed or conviction. The Palstra family was sent from country to country as Salvation Army missionaries, spending a few years in each location before being moved on. Will's father Wiebe kept being promoted. By the time the family arrived in Melbourne, The Salvation Army had been established there for 30 years.

In 1912 the Army's newspaper, *The War Cry*, reported the arrival in Melbourne of the steamship *Marathon* and its passengers, including 'the new Chief Secretary for the Commonwealth of Australia, Colonel Wiebe Palstra and Mrs. Palstra and their seven children'. The newspaper published 'Colonel' and Mrs. Palstra's portraits on the front cover, alongside drawings of windmills, clogs and African tribesman brandishing spears, to illustrate how ethnically rich and extraordinary their missionary travels had been.

In fact, the eldest of those seven children had been left behind in England. The Salvation Army had not agreed to twenty-one-year-old William Palstra's request to be transferred with his family, and he was forced to remain at International Headquarters in London where he worked as an office clerk, with the rank of 'captain'.

From the very start, Will had done his utmost to persuade his employers to include him in the family transfer, but his pleas fell on deaf ears. In a letter to his parents on 26th August 1912, just before their departure for Australia, he had written,

> 'I can quite see that in the Army it is necessary to sacrifice a lot, and we do. It is because we get so used to these sacrifices that we seem almost to take them for granted. That the authorities should however have power to break up families at will I somehow cannot quite agree with. I cannot quite contemplate the idea of parting with you in this way...'

Will was torn between being honest about his feelings while not giving his parents cause to worry about him. He added the following lines to his letter, couched in the 'fighting' terminology of The Salvation Army:

> '... yet I do not doubt for one moment that in some way or other, the Lord who has looked after us in a truly marvellous manner all these years, will provide a way, and everything will turn out alright. In that hope, I live and fight on.'

On the day of their departure from England he stood on the pier amongst a crowd of Salvation Army well-wishers and watched the *Marathon* steam away, carrying his beloved family to the other side of the world. No doubt he waved to them until they dwindled from view. That afternoon he returned to his lodgings, alone and desolate.

Front cover of The Salvation Army's '*War Cry*' newspaper, 14th December 1912, announcing the arrival in Australia of Will's family.

Will missed them all desperately—his loving parents, his sisters Henrietta and Blanche, and his brothers Charles, Frank, Victor and John. He tried to cope with the separation, but as months passed it became even harder to bear. The young man's efficiency and devotion to his job had not worked in his favour; Headquarters considered him indispensable. He was a valuable addition to the staff of the London office and they were not prepared to pay his fare to Melbourne.

For Will, three bulwarks stood steadfast and trustworthy amidst the stormy ocean of life's uncertainties: family, Christianity and the British Empire. Though he would question them all, at various times and to various degrees, he never dreamed of forswearing any of them. To the bitter end, he would never surrender so much as the tiniest particle of loyalty to his kindred, his faith and Britannia.

Now for the first time he began to question the institution that had shaped his entire life thus far. It was not The Salvation Army's ideals he impugned, but their bureaucracy.

If the Army would not transfer him, the only other option was to resign and undertake the voyage on his own, as a private citizen. For Will, born and raised as a dedicated 'Soldier of the Cross', leaving the Army's employ seemed like a last resort. He was well aware, too, that his father and mother were keen for him to continue his career with the Army and their opinion was of the greatest importance to the young man. He strove, all his life, to make them proud of him.

And there was another hurdle—with his low salary, no matter how thriftily he lived, he would not be able to save enough money for the fare. His yearning for reunion with his family weighed heavily on him. Furthermore, his interest in that remote land of Australia was deepening for, as he wrote to his father in a note accompanying a birthday present,

> 'My ideas, as one who views from afar, is that it must be a country with unbounded possibilities in every way.'

The Palstra family circa 1912: L to R back row: Frank, Will, Wiebe (father), Charles, Victor. Centre: Hettie, Jacoba (mother). Front row: John, Blanche.

Will's father and mother understood the situation. They wrote to him that if he were left with no option but to resign, they would send him the money for a ticket to Australia.

In May 1914 Will was still pining away in London when, while tidying up his commanding officer's papers one morning, he chanced upon a personal note to the Colonel from Commissioner Whatmore, asking whether he had 'yet spoken to Captain Palstra about Java'.

A transfer to Java! This came as a shock. It was clear that the Army could happily dispense with his services in London and afford to pay his fare to Indonesia, but they refused to send him to Australia where he so desperately yearned to go!

This was the final straw. Will's sense of betrayal and unfair treatment, combined with his desperate need for family reunion, drove him to make a decision which was for him, at that time, monumental. He would resign from The Salvation Army staff.

Just before he was ready to make his move, war broke out in Europe. This did not change Will's intentions one iota. He resigned from his position as 'Private Shorthand and Secretary' on the staff at the International Headquarters of The Salvation Army, thus losing his rank of 'captain' and, at the age of twenty-three, travelled to Australia.

Will's voyage from London, on board the P&O steamship *Beltana*, took more than six weeks. He arrived in Melbourne during the closing days of September, 1914.

His joy at being back with his family was somewhat marred, however—for, while he was crossing the seas, the newly formed Australian Imperial Force (AIF) had commenced recruiting, and his brother Charles, a twenty-one year old clerk, had enlisted. His parents were proud of his enterprise, but even as Will strode down the gangway onto Australian shores, his arms outstretched to embrace those dear ones who waited for him on the pier, he must have noted the strain and worry on their faces, thinly disguised by their smiles of welcome. The entire family had suffered the pangs of seeing a son and brother march off to become a soldier.

1915: A Victorian Clerk | 2: The Outbreak of the Great War

It was on Tuesday 4 August, 1914, that Great Britain, head of an empire so vast that it covered a quarter of Earth's total land area, declared war on Germany.

Rumours of war had been brewing for months, and in the weeks leading up to the declaration the whole world seemed breathless with suspense, awaiting an official announcement. The swiftest mode of international communication was by electric telegraph. A telegram, or 'cable', could take only a matter of hours—as opposed to weeks by steamship—to travel from England to Australia, on the other side of the world.[3]

In London, at 11pm on that Tuesday, a telegraph operator received a written message from the Secretary of State for the Colonies. He translated the momentous news into Morse

---

3 Intercontinental telegrams worked by the sending of electrical signals along submarine telegraph cables, using Morse code. At the other end of the line Morse code experts translated the coded signals into words, typed them on paper and sent them by messenger or post to the recipient. The link between Australia and England passed between several repeater stations, and along cables that went under the sea between Darwin and Java, and from there overland across the continent.

code, tapping out the sequence of long and short pulses into a transmitter—dot-dash-dot-dash, beep-beep . . .

Southeast the electrical signals travelled, along miles of overland cables, across the continent of Europe and down through India, passing through repeater stations that boosted their strength. Across the breadth of India they flew, before diving below the Bay of Bengal, headed for Singapore. From there the coded message was relayed to Indonesia and after plunging beneath the Timor Sea it finally touched the Australian continent at that northern outpost, the city of Darwin.

Australia's Overland Telegraph system seized the signals, pumping them southwards to Melbourne, the home of the Australian Federal Parliament. Within minutes they reached their destination, where an operator decoded them into words on paper. Before noon that day, 5th August, a postal messenger entered the office of the Governor General of Australia and handed him the telegram.

Soon afterwards, at the hubs of the busily murmuring cable networks, newspaper offices erupted into sudden activity. The great metal rollers of the printing presses thundered to life, churning out the news: ENGLAND DECLARES WAR AGAINST GERMANY. It is worth quoting the reports here, because they convey so well the sense of excitement and patriotic fervour that swirled through the whole country. In an era before television, journalists had to use wordcraft to evoke vivid images in the minds of the readers.

The Age, 5 August 1914

```
AUSTRALIANS JOIN THE WAR AS TRUE BRITONS

Great Britain and the Empire are at war with Germany. Our
Prime Minister, Mr Cook, has already pledged our loyalty.
In fierce fighting words he said tonight: "Our resources are
great and the British spirit is not dead . . . Our duty is
quite clear - namely to gird up our loins and remember that
we are Britons."
```

All over Australia, the declaration of war was causing a stir. In Melbourne it was as if, rather than a war, a party had been declared.

To Australians, Britain had always been 'the mother country'. She was called 'home', even by those who had never set foot on her shores, and Australians were proud to call themselves citizens of the British Empire.

***The Argus* Melbourne, Thursday 6 August 1914, Page 6**

```
SCENES IN THE CITY.

WAR NEWS RELIEVES TENSION.

GERMAN CONSULATE DESERTED.

Strained expectancy, rather than enthusiasm, was the keynote
of the people's feelings yesterday morning. The streets
were exceptionally crowded . . .

By half past 12 a dense mass of people waiting for the issue
of the extraordinary edition extended from the footpath to
the tram-track outside "The Argus" office. Elderly Gentlemen
and professional men were as eager to be up near the door as
were the newspaper runners, and a certain amount of pushing
from the rear of the crowd pressed those in front right into
the door-way.

With arms locked, several policemen on the steps made heroic
efforts to stem the tide, but it was not until reinforcements
arrived that the people were driven back off the pavement.
There was no rowdyism — only an intense desire to learn the
latest news of the situation. The minutes dragged by, and
the excitement of the crowd grew almost feverish. "What's
the news?" "Tell us the news," shouted an impatient man at
the back of the crowd, and a hundred other voices took up
the call.

At last the signal was given to admit the eager mob, and
an extraordinary scene ensued. The police made strenuous
efforts to admit the crowd in small batches, but their efforts
```

were in vain. A seething crowd broke through the cordon at the door and rushed the counter where the papers were being sold. The noise as the would-be purchasers shouted the number of copies they wished to obtain was simply deafening, and conjured up descriptions of the wheat pit in Chicago during the recent panic.

In an incredibly short time after the first copy had been sold, everyone in the street seemed to have heard the news of the declaration of war. Some were enthusiastic, some evidently gratified: some seemed overweighted by the import of the news, some were openly pessimistic. But the general feeling was one of relief, that the terrible waiting and uncertainty of the last few days was over, and that, whatever the issue might be Great Britain had made her voice known in the quarrel of the nations.

During the morning the German consul "left" Melbourne, that important diplomatic formality being achieved by unscrewing the name-plate from the consulate door and whitewashing the windows. A few cases of Germans, or supposed Germans, being hustled by the crowd were reported, but as far as could be ascertained no actual injury was caused.

Similar scenes of enthusiasm to those of Tuesday were enacted in the cafes in town. The bands played snatches of patriotic tunes, and the patrons, rising to their feet, joined fervently in the choruses.

An air of gaiety pervaded the Spencer Street Platform at the departure of the Sydney express yesterday. Numbers of passengers wore national emblems of England and France. A small group of French people chatted incessantly before entering a first-class compartment. One enthusiast in the party began singing "God Save the King" and the rest joined in, the ladies waving flags. A few naval reservists also left for Sydney, and were farewelled by friends. As the train moved off cheers resounded all along the platform, and responding ovations were given by passengers.

At both the J.C. Williamson Limited's theatres, Her Majesty and the Theatre Royal, there were scenes of enthusiasm last night. The National Anthem was played by the orchestras prior to the rising of the curtain, and on the conclusion of "The Mikado" and "A Royal Divorce" both the artists on the stage and the audience joined in the singing of "God Save the King", a stirring patriotic demonstration following.

For some people, the tension spilled into violence.

The Age, Melbourne, 5 August 1914

ENORMOUS CROWDS.
EXTRAORDINARY ENTHUSIASM.
WILD CHEERING AND PATRIOTIC SONGS.

Scenes of wild enthusiasm were witnessed outside "The Age" office last night. All day long and throughout the early part of the evening there was always a crowd extending out on to the road reading the cables as they were posted up [telegrams displayed on public noticeboards outside the newspaper offices], but as the hour grew late, so the crowd grew denser, and spread right across Collins-street. It needed only a single voice to give the opening bars of a patriotic song, and thousands of throats took it up, hats and coats were waved, and those who were lucky enough to possess even the smallest of Union Jacks were the heroes of the moment, and were raised shoulder high as the crowd surged hither and thither. "Rule Britannia", "Soldiers of The King", and "Sons of the Sea" were sung again and again. The National Anthem ["God Save the King"] had a sobering effect from time to time, and woe betide anyone who failed to remove his hat without hesitation. Suddenly a Frenchman got up on the steps and commenced singing the Marseillaise. The crowd grew frantic with enthusiasm. He was lifted bodily in the air shouting, "Vive l'Angleterre !" "Vive la France!"

A mention of Germany caused an irresponsible youth to shout, "Let's go and wreck the consul's office!" The cry was taken up probably by the "hoodlum" element in the throng, and for a few minutes there was an ugly feeling displayed. The timely arrival of a Scottish piper diverted attention, and he became the object of attention. The police allowed him to march up and down directly in front of the office, but the pipes could be but dimly heard through the cheering and yelling.

About 11.33 p.m., in response to the persistent cry of "We want more news," a notice was put up stating that there would be no more news that night.

"We won't go home till morning!" shouted someone, and every voice took up the chorus. Suddenly two blue jackets [navy sailors] arrived on the scene and they were pounced upon. A procession was formed, and they were carried up and down the street to the tune of "Rule Britannia", "Boys of the Bulldog Breed", and "Sons of the Sea". Finally the procession, or part of it, marched up the steps of the office, deposited the jovial tars on the counter, and asked, "Is there any more war news?" The notice already posted was confirmed, and the crowd gradually dwindled away, though at midnight there were still some hundreds in the street, determined to wait till the decision of the British Cabinet could be made known.

The British dominions, including Canada and New Zealand, pledged to send troops to the aid of the motherland. Australia promised to send 20,000 men.

Most Australians had unshakeable confidence in British superiority and infallibility. Journalists and editors across the country published articles about allegiance to the Empire and the importance of marshalling to support the cause.

On Thursday 6th August *The Argus* proclaimed:
> ```
> The patience and the sincerity with which the King and
> his advisors [have negotiated with Germany] have failed,
> but their indirect effect has been to unite the Empire as
> it never was united before in a determination to stand
> beside the old land to help her through any agonies ... if
> necessary, the last man and the last shilling.
> 
> There is great excitement in the armed forces and men are
> rushing to join up . . .
> ```

The first shot fired in anger by any armed force of the British Empire, including Great Britain, was from the gunners of Fort Nepean, at the entrance to Port Phillip Bay in Victoria, just fifty-six miles from Melbourne by road. It happened just three hours and forty-five minutes after war was declared in London.

At dawn on Thursday 6 August Melbourne time, the German freighter *SS Pfalz* had been steaming rapidly towards Port Phillip Heads, when news reached Fort Queenscliff that war had begun. Immediately, orders were sent to the coastal battery at Fort Nepean by telephone and heliograph to stop the Pfalz from leaving the bay. Five minutes later the fort fired a single round. The cannonball tore across the bows of the SS Pfalz and splashed harmlessly beneath the waves. After a brief struggle on the bridge between the German captain and the Australian pilot, Captain Robinson, Captain Kuhlken surrendered and the Pfalz was taken into captivity.

The Great War had commenced.

In a constitutional sense, the Commonwealth of Australia was automatically at war immediately Britain declared hostilities. Yet there was much more to it than that. With the outbreak of war, Australians were roused to an unprecedented outpouring of nationalistic fervour. The nation was less than fourteen years old, but it wanted to burst into flower with a vengeance.

Before 1914 Australia didn't really have much of an army. The defence force consisted mainly of the Citizens' Militia, which was restricted to service within Australian territory.

At the outbreak of war, however, Great Britain's dominions were eager to give their utmost, to unreservedly make any sacrifice to support 'the cause of Empire'. The following newspaper article demonstrates the extent of Australia's commitment:

The Argus, **Melbourne, Tuesday, August 4. 1914**

In making so prompt an offer to send troops to the assistance of the mother-land in the emergency confronting her, the Commonwealth Government has risen splendidly to a great occasion. Australia is now in line with Canada and New Zealand and, with those dominions, will be prepared to stretch her resources to the uttermost in the cause of Empire.

It is an inspiring thing, this eager loyalty of the oversea Britons and the moral effect of it cannot but be very great. Great Britain's value as an ally or a friend and her formidableness as an enemy must be enormously magnified. It shows that British strength is not to be estimated by the number of the people or the amount of treasures to be found within the United Kingdom, but that every community living under the flag is not only willing but eager to do its utmost in the common cause.

The Imperial impulse which sent out contingent after contingent of colonial troops to South Africa is moving us again and more strongly than ever. For there is this time a sterner foe to be matched and a greater danger to be faced. It is felt that the very existence of the Empire may depend on the issue of the struggle which has commenced in Europe. The discomfiture of Great Britain's friends would derange the balance upon which the liberties of Europe are at this moment based and no one cares to surmise what the ultimate consequences might be.

> What Australia can do, and will do should the necessity arise, is not to be measured by the present offer to hand over the fleet and to despatch 20,000 men. That is merely an instalment, an earnest of the efforts and the sacrifices she is prepared to make. Neither men nor money will be wanting, let the toll be never so frequent. And the certain gain will be greater than all possible loss.
>
> That the Commonwealth Government should at the same moment be placing the warships of the Australian fleet unconditionally at the disposal of the Imperial authorities is no more than was expected. Whether the [British] Admiralty decides to retain them in these seas or to summon them to Europe with all haste, Australian opinion will be equally favourable.
>
> The one thing of importance is to entrust unreservedly to the authority responsible for the safety and the interests of the Empire us a whole whatever military and naval resources we have at our disposal. If the Admiralty thinks proper to add the vessels of the Australian fleet unit to its present strength in home waters, it may rest assured of our confidence in the wisdom of its plans.
>
> The Australian people are wise enough to wish to see their warships employed to the utmost possible advantage. There need be no fear, therefore, that they will challenge or carp at any decision the Admiralty may come to in regard to the disposition of their fleet.

People believed that while the war in Europe might be very distant, it was a war in which Australia and New Zealand were fighting for their very existence.

Since about ninety-eight per cent of the population could claim British birth or origin, most Australians felt that whatever happened to Britain was, in a way, also happening to Australia.

Montague Grover, editor of the *Sydney Sun*, 31 October 1914

```
'Our own national existence, our security as the people to
inhabit and control this continent, will disappear if Germany
wins. We are not merely "helping Britain" - a phrase used
as though we claimed the credit of some generous sacrifices
- but are fighting for ourselves. Britain is helping us in
at least the same degree. Our security abides or vanishes
along with hers.

With the downfall of British sea-supremacy Australia could
have no such confidence, but could at any moment become a
foreign nation's prey. That very downfall is Germany's
purpose in the war. For Britain it would mean disaster
approaching ruin, but for Australia its menace would be
national extinction.'
```

If Australia were to participate in the Great War, a separate all-volunteer force had to be recruited specifically for overseas service. The Australian government's pledge of full support for Britain led to the raising of the Australian Imperial Force—the AIF.

Recruiting started on 10 August. Such was the enthusiasm with which Australians volunteered at the beginning of the war, that an entire battalion could be raised within two weeks. By November 1914, after only two months of basic training, twenty thousand Australian soldiers, accompanied by New Zealand troops, were on their way across the sea, bound for the other side of the world.

Charles Palstra, who had enlisted on 17 August, was among them. Aged 22 years and 7 months, he was described on his application form as 5 feet 8 inches tall (172 cm) with blue eyes, fair skin and brown hair.

No doubt it was the contagious 'war fever' that made young Charles join the AIF. Large numbers of young men were flocking to sign up. Charles, like nearly everyone in 1914, probably didn't think the war would last long. Most of the recruits believed they'd be home by Christmas. Enlistment, too, was a matter of pride and self-respect. Young unmarried chaps who didn't enlist were sometimes derided as 'would-to-godders'. A would-to-godder was a civilian who 'would to God that he could go to the war', only he was prevented from doing so by failing the medical examination or some such hindrance that was not given much credibility by some members of the public.

Private Lynch, author of *Somme Mud*, wrote:

> No one ever seems to admit that he enlisted out of love of country, or because he thought his loved ones were in danger. Somehow it seems that most of us enlisted because our mates did. That men were driven to enlist by that urging spirit of pulling together that is really mateship undefined. A man enlists because his mates do, not because he wants to bayonet and bomb other men.[4]

When Charles Palstra filled out the enlistment form, he wrote down his father as his 'next of kin', but he Anglicised his father's name from 'Wiebe' to 'William', just to be on the safe side. This might have been a canny move on his part. It is not unlikely that people wondered whether 'Colonel' Palstra was German, as soon as they heard his given name. Ever since the outbreak of war, people with German-sounding names had been reviled. Even the names of some Australian towns had been changed on that basis. 'Colonel' Palstra's name was Dutch, not German, but in Australia the distinction might have been viewed as minimal. After all, both Holland[5] and Germany were distant European countries whose inhabitants spoke a foreign language.

---

4   Private Edward Francis Lynch (1897 – 12 September 1980) First AIF.

5   The family referred to 'Holland' in their letters, rather than 'The Netherlands'.

By the time Will arrived in Melbourne, Charles Palstra was stationed at his military training camp. On the twenty-first of October, only a month later, the eager young soldier departed with his comrades on active service, sailing on the troopship *Orvieto* from Melbourne's Station Pier with his unit—the Fifth Battalion, Second Brigade, First Australian Division. Both the First Division and the Light Horse were bound for Egypt, which was under British control.

Charles Palstra could not know it, but he was destined to become part of Australian history as an Anzac.

1915: A Victorian Clerk | 3: The Anzacs

Stir up the feeling for defence, boys!
Stir it up with might and main!
We'll fight for the Empire and the Land we love,
And take the place of brothers who are slain.
We've put aside our cricket and our football,
We're coming with the rifle and the gun;
We're bringing lots of chaps to fill those vacant gaps,
For we are soldiers—every one.[6]

Who were the Anzacs?

In the early days of the war, New Zealand mustered insufficient infantry battalions to form their own division, while Australia did not have enough recruits to form a second division. In Egypt, the Australians combined with the New Zealanders to form a corps

---

6   Verse from, 'Wake up! Australia, An Appeal from the Dardanelles'. Music by Alfred Mansfield, 1897. Published by the Stanley Mullen Company, 1915. Melbourne: Aberdeen Buildings, 528-530 Collins St. Sydney: Macdonell House, 315-321 Pitt St.

under the command of New Zealand's Major-General Alexander Godley. This fighting unit, the Australian and New Zealand Army Corps, was known as ANZAC.

'Six bob a day tourists,' some called them, those enthusiastic volunteers of 1914. It was a term of derision, based on the supposition that these young men expected the war to end before they were fit to take the field, and had therefore enlisted merely for the pay and the opportunity to travel. It would be less than a year before any derision was well and truly wiped away by the events that followed.

Charles Palstra and the Fifth Battalion arrived in the Middle East on 2 December 1914. On the hot desert sands, beneath the gaze of the majestic pyramids, they trained with the British Army's Mediterranean Expeditionary Force[7], making ready for service on the Western Front.

Christmas passed, and a new year began. By then, back in Australia, Will had found employment at the Pianola Company. He was content, earning a steady—if small—income, and living with his family.

Early in February 1915 Charles's brigade took part in the defence of the Suez Canal, in which the Turks failed to take the canal from the British. The Palstra family was beset by worry, and Charles was always in their prayers. The same month the British government's War Council decided that instead of proceeding to the Western Front, the Australians and New Zealanders would take part in an assault on the straits of the Dardanelles[8] which, they confidently predicted, would knock Turkey out of the war.

It came to be called 'the Gallipoli Campaign'.

---

7   Lieutenant-General Sir William Birdwood was the Commander of the Mediterranean Expeditionary Force. Field Marshal Lord Kitchener was Commander in Chief of the British Army.

8   The Dardanelles is a narrow strait in north-western Turkey connecting the Aegean Sea to the Sea of Marmara. In 1915, the western Allies sent a massive invasion force of British, Indian, Australian, and New Zealand troops to attempt to open up the strait. At the Gallipoli campaign, Turkish troops trapped the Allies on the beaches of the Gallipoli peninsula.

The propaganda posters of the Great War depicted battle in a sanitised mode. It was important to keep up the public's morale. Charles's family and friends would have been given a sketchy idea of what happened at Gallipoli. Only those who had experienced battle first-hand knew the truth.

On Sunday 25 April 1915 Charles' battalion was part of the ANZAC landing, under heavy fire, on the beach at Gallipoli.

The landing, on the promontory of Gaba Tepe, took place just before dawn. The enemy had spotted the Australians and rained fire on the smaller boats as they approached the beach. The Fifth were coming in to shore in the troopship *Novian*, with the brigade staff. The vessel had some difficulty in getting to her berth, and when she reached it no tows or destroyers came to her, so the Fifth were much later in landing than the Sixth and the Seventh.

The pre-dawn light was growing, and the beach was also lit by the glare from bursting shells. From their ship Private Charles Palstra and his mates would have commanded a fairly good view of the scene on the water as the Sixth and Seventh landed.

The larger launches and pinnaces grounded in deeper water, whereupon the men tumbled over the bows or the sides, often falling on the slippery stones, so that it was hard to say who was hit by bullets and who was not. Some, barely noticed in the rush, slipped into water too deep for them. The heavy kit that a man carried just sank him like a stone. Some were grabbed by a comrade who happened to observe them; one was hung up by his kit on a rowlock.

Young men died in the water, before they even reached the shore. Some were killed while still in their boats. After sorrowful leave-takings from their mothers, after all their training and careful preparation and packing, after the long distance they'd travelled over the sea, they had fallen before they even fired a shot for their cause.

All of this, Charles would have had no choice but to witness. He, a Salvation Army boy, an office clerk, had never seen such a bloodbath. Before he even stepped into the landing boat, he beheld agony, death and destruction on an unimaginable scale.

With the Fifth, Charles came ashore in the second wave of boats, bearing witness to the ghastly fate of the first, and receiving the same treatment at the hands of the enemy.

They landed around seven o'clock that morning. Bullets were striking sparks out of the shingle as the boatloads reached the shore. Men fell by the score, shot down before they could wade to land. The shore ran crimson with blood. Those who landed raced across the sand, the bullets striking sparks at their feet, and flung themselves down, as instructed, in the shelter of the sandy bank—which in some places amounted to nothing more than a low cliff—where the hillside ended and the beach began.

A high, rugged slope pressed down to the beach. Fierce rifle-fire swept over the men lying in little parties of boatloads and platoons, out of sight of most of their comrades, their clothes heavy with water, and their rifles choked with sand.

On land, the fire was increasing fast. Machine-guns were barking from invisible positions above. Company after company, battalion after battalion moved into the fight, pressing forward uphill, climbing the steep plateau while swept relentlessly by machine gun fire and shells.

Even as Private Charles Palstra disembarked, bullets tore through his foot and arm. He fell, there on the beach among his comrades, beneath the metal hail of death.

But—so far—he was one of the lucky ones. Though racked with agony, he still lived.

The ADMS[9] First Australian Division landed with divisional headquarters at half past seven. By that time, chaos reigned. Wounded men were accumulating on the beach and disposal became an urgent matter. By 10.30 a.m. the Casualty Clearing Station was established and by noon they were hard at work attending the wounded, Charles Palstra included.

---

9   Assistant Director Medical Services

The National Museum of Australia records: 'For the vast majority of the 16,000 Australians and New Zealanders who landed on that day, it was their first experience of combat. By that evening, 2,000 of them had been killed or wounded.'

Examiner **(Launceston, Tasmania)Monday 24 May 1915 Page 6**

```
Australian casualty lists

WOUNDED IN ACTION

VICTORIA

Pte. C. E. Palstra . . .
```

Reports of the carnage at Gallipoli caused shockwaves when they reached Australia. The men who enlisted in the AIF after this date would be called the 'fair dinkums'; because unlike the first lot, they knew what they were getting themselves into.

'Gallipoli' was the first major military action fought by Australian and New Zealand forces during the Great War. The bloody, heroic, terrible battle on that initial day, in that place, struck so deeply into the Australian and New Zealand psyche that both governments decreed that a day of national remembrance would thenceforth be held annually. On 30 April 1915, when the first news of the landing reached New Zealand, a half-day holiday was declared in honour of the fallen, and across the country impromptu memorial services were held. The news made the same profound impact on Australians when they learned what had happened, and 25 April quickly became a day of remembrance.[10]

The Gallipoli campaign lasted from 25 April 1915 to 20 December 1915.

Charlie Palstra survived the long and appalling day of the landing in the midst of that hail of bullets, shrapnel and shells. Hot metal missiles had struck him in the right foot and the right arm. The wounds were not mortal, but they must have become infected, for a week

---

10 In Australia, ANZAC Day became a holiday in 1925. In each state it was declared a National Day of Remembrance in the Commonwealth ANZAC Day Act 1995.

later, on 2 May, he was admitted to the 1st Australian General Hospital at Heliopolis, in Cairo, Egypt.

Back in Australia the family rejoiced and thanked God when they received the news of Charlie's survival and removal from the front line.

On 19th June Charles was deemed fit enough to be transferred from Egypt to a hospital in England, aboard the ship *Nevasa*. Months later the Australian newspapers were still reporting on his battalion, which was still serving at 'Anzac', enduring severe hardship as they held the beachhead, with no end to the stalemate in sight.

1915: A Victorian Clerk | 4: Family Life

March on, Salvation Soldiers, march forward to the fight,

With Jesus as our leader, we'll put the foe to flight;

In spite of men and devils we'll raise our banner high,

For the day of victory's coming by and by.[11]

Having achieved his goal of joining his family in Australia, Will seems to have been content with his lot in life. There is nothing to suggest that he was anything other than happy to be a hard-working office clerk from a family which, though of excellent character and reputation, set no great store by making any more money than was needed for the bare necessities of life. It appears that as long as he was surrounded by his loved ones, he was perfectly content with the status quo, despite having lost his Salvation Army title of 'captain'

---

11   The Day of Victory's Coming. James Conner Bateman (1855-88)

and his role as a 'soldier of the cross', along with the familiar, military-style uniform that accompanied it.

There was an informality among the inhabitants of his newly-adopted country that he had not encountered in the 'old world'. It seemed to Will that this was a land of limitless possibilities, unfettered by class distinctions; a country in which a man could achieve great heights if he worked hard. Enlistment was the last thing on his mind.

Number 1 Walker Street, Northcote, was the Palstra family's second home since they had first set foot in Australia. As members of The Salvation Army, whose job it was to spread the Word, the family was used to rootlessness and moving from place to place, never owning any real estate. It was the Army who determined which country would be their home for a few years, whereabouts in that country they would live, and how many those years would be.

Not long after Will's arrival, however, the household had moved from their first house in East Malvern, and the Palstras now lived in a weatherboard house at 1 Walker Street, Northcote, on a corner[12] overlooking Merri Creek.

Imagine him arriving home from work that Saturday.

The rose bushes along the fence, which he pruned a few weeks earlier, are in bud. Smoke is rising from the kitchen chimney. He enters through the side gate and heads for the back door, passing by the outdoor latrine and the canvas tent that stands in the back yard to provide sleeping quarters for two of his brothers, the house being too small for such a large family. His mother's chickens are clucking and pecking in their coop near the vegetable patch, while laundered garments flap on the clothes-line.

Will's seventeen-year-old sister Blanche is unpegging the clean clothes and dropping them into a large wicker basket. A breeze tousles her long, blonde locks, and the hem of her dress whips at her ankles. She waves at the new arrival, and he calls out to her.

---

12   The house at #1 Walker Street still existed as of February 2014, and could then be seen on Google Street View.

Frank, nineteen, and a bank clerk by profession, is chopping wood for the fire, his singlet blotched with perspiration. He looks up. 'Hello, old chap!' he says, wiping his brow with the back of his hand.

In the kitchen, Will's mother greets him with a fond peck on the cheek. A small, dainty woman with fair hair greying at the temples, she is wearing a faded apron over her Salvation Army uniform. Seated at the kitchen table, twenty-three year old Hettie, a teacher by profession, is helping their youngest brother, John, with his schoolwork. Will kisses his sister on the forehead and ruffles John's hair. 'How are you, Jock?' By the rowdy blare of a cornet emanating from elsewhere in the house it is clear that Victor, aged fifteen, is rehearsing 'Onward, Christian Soldiers'.

Will's father, 'Colonel' Palstra, is probably still in his office at Territorial Headquarters in the city, where he works long hours.

Dad was often late home, even on Saturdays. Not for him a working week of a mere forty-eight hours—like most senior Salvation Army officers he kept his 'nose to the grindstone' as long as there were tasks to be done.

Will treasured the times he spent with his father. This man, whom he admired and respected above all others, had almost died of smallpox when Will was only six years old and the family lived in Brussels. Dad was his closest friend and confidante, and he loved him with utmost filial devotion. The two of them enjoyed each other's company, often indulging in quiet chats on philosophical, spiritual or mundane topics. He welcomed Dad's words of advice and encouragement and felt intellectually stimulated by their exchange of ideas.

It must have felt like a blessing that 'Colonel' Palstra was in Melbourne at all. As second-in-command of The Salvation Army in Australia, he was on the executive board and in charge of the administrative side of the Army's work. When Commissioner James Hay was absent, he became acting Territorial Commander. He was often away for days or weeks on end, having received many invitations to officiate at a wide variety of events around Australia or to give his popular lectures on 'The Part played by Great Britain in the War' and 'The Salvation Army and its Work Among the Troops'.

Part II
1915: The Bugles of England

1915: The Bugles of England | 1: The Hero's Return

Australia's sons are noble, they're noble and they're true;

Their hearts are stout and fearless and pure as morning dew,

And for freedom, home and kindred, and Australia ever dear,

They faced the fiercest foemen with hearts that knew no fear.

And far away across the brine, far o'er the raging foam,

Far from Australia's sunny clime, far from their native home,

Their courage did not falter, they sprang into the sea,

And waded through the water straight for Gallipoli.

The world was filled with wonder as they bravely breast the main,

While Turkish guns did thunder and bullets showered like rain.

Gallipoli's rugged coast-line did lift the lid of hell,

And the story of that landing no pen or tongue can tell.

But onward! Onward o'er the waves surged forth that gallant band,

And some of them found watery graves, whilst others reached the land.

Up yonder hill they sped, the foeman's doom to seal,

They thought of comrades dead, and freely used the steel.

And soon the foe were flying, as Australia's "Coo-ee" rang,

And amid the dead and dying lay many a Turk and Hun.

And now the story will be told, for never can it fade,

Inscribe it in the purest gold. The charge Australians made. [13]

September's days blew away with the last pale petals from the fruit trees in the Walker Street backyard. October brought news of the happiest sort. On the eighth—Will's twenty-fourth birthday—Charlie Palstra would be embarking from Plymouth, England, aboard

---

13   'The Charge Australians Made', by 'Gumsucker'. Music by A. C. Quinn. Published by M. Keogh, 6 Elizabeth St., Norwood, Sth Australia, 1915.

HMAT[14] *Suavic*, a White Star Liner which in wartime operated as a troop carrier under the British Navy's Liner Requisition Scheme.

The *Suavic* carried soldiers who were coming home because they had been rendered unfit for active service, whether by injury or disease. Charles, still a private in the Fifth Battalion, First Division, was fully healed from his injuries and would be on duty as a ship's guard.

It would only be for a visit, with ten days' leave, but he was coming home!

All over the country, people were talking about the glorious heroism and sacrifice of the Australian soldiers fighting abroad. Thousands of young men had fallen; thousands more had been wounded. Songs, poems and marches were composed in their honour.

Appeals to Australian men to enlist screamed from newspapers and recruitment posters. Recruiting marches were held throughout New South Wales and Queensland. A riderless horse was led through the streets of Australian towns to the beat of a military drum. 'The Empire needs you! Who will fill the saddle?'

Numbers of young men known to the Palstras joined the AIF and sailed away on heavily-laden troop ships, cheered and farewelled by vast crowds thronging Melbourne's Station Pier.

For many families, every day that passed without receiving one of the dreaded telegrams from the Department of Defence was another day they could cling to hope that eventually their boys would come home.

The Palstra family waited for Charles, praying for a safe voyage for *Suavic*. Meanwhile, every day was crammed with the usual activities. In addition to Salvation Army administration, fund raising and social occasions, there was always work to be done among the homeless, the unemployed, the mentally ill, the disabled, and people struggling with addictions and poverty.

At last the longed-for moment arrived. On Sunday, 19 November 1915, Private Charles Palstra's ship docked at Station Pier, welcomed by wildly cheering onlookers crowding the wharf. A stream of young soldiers began pouring from the vessel—some leaning on

---

14   His Majesty's Australian Transport

walking-sticks, others with bandaged heads, eye-patches or arms in slings, many on crutches or being pushed in wheelchairs, or borne on stretchers.

As Charles walked down the gangway among the patients he must have cut a dashing figure in his army uniform; the khaki jacket, loose-necked and finished with black metal buttons; the baggy woollen trousers, the sturdy, lace-up, ankle-length boots, their soles hobnailed for extra grip. There were no medals gleaming above his heart, because the Star, the British War Medal and the Victory Medal had not yet been issued.[15] Like his comrades, however, Charles wore his peaked service cap pinned with its shining badge of the 'rising sun', and another badge of the same design on his collar. His epaulettes bore his battalion number, the letters INF (infantry) and the word 'Australia' embroidered in an arc. He carried his kit bag slung over his shoulder.

At last Charles, having handed over his charges to the local military police, is released from guard duty and pushes through the dockside crowds to find his family. Picture the scene that then unfolded.

'Thanks be to the Lord! You look wonderful my boy!' 'Colonel' Palstra welcomes his son, shaking his hand with fervent exhilaration. Like his wife, he is clad in the black Salvation Army uniform.

Jacoba reaches up and throws her arms around her boy. Her eyes are moist. 'Charlie, it is so good to see you!'

Amidst the noisy, milling throng, the young Anzac greets his family, each in turn, embracing the girls and shaking hands with the boys. Blanche links her arm with his. Frank insists on shouldering his haversack. Hettie and Victor pelt him with questions while John stares up at his older brother in open-mouthed admiration. Will is beaming. Everyone is happy, and his beloved family is whole again. He takes in the sight of this soldier, so different from the younger brother he had last seen in London in 1912.

---

15   Furthermore, the Anzac Commemorative Medallion would not be conceived of until fifty years later.

What an impressive sight Charlie Palstra presented; the sun-tanned Anzac wearing a real army uniform instead of the ersatz military costume of The Salvation Army. And what encomiums he was receiving—from strangers and friends, from his siblings, from his mother and above all—Will notices—from Dad.

As for Charles, who could know what he was truly thinking and feeling, after the hell he'd been through? Who could know what demons plagued his nightmares?

Charles had departed as an unworldly, fresh-faced young man and returned as a battle-scarred hero. A joyful bevy of family members and friends escorted him through the throng to the railway station, where they caught the train home.

Charles was pleased to reveal that he had been selected to study for a commission at the highly-esteemed Royal Military College (RMC) of Duntroon, in Australia's new capital city of Canberra. At Duntroon, cadets graduated as second lieutenants,[16] with a star upon their shoulders. When they had proved their worth in the field they would be promoted to the full rank of lieutenant, and command a platoon of forty-three men.

Imagine 'Colonel' Wiebe Palstra's eyes shining with pride as he looked upon his second-born son, and how he would have praised the young man's achievements and bright future, in front of the whole family.

On Charles's return home he became the vortex of a social whirlpool. The family could not do enough for him. Indeed, the whole world seemed to esteem him. Men in AIF uniform were honoured as heroes. Even strangers in the street would smile and wave, calling out, 'Good on yer, Anzac!' [17] At Salvation Army gatherings, people flocked around him. Every citizen was passionately proud of the Australian and New Zealand armed forces.

---

16   Lieutenant: Pronounced 'leftenant' in Australia, as in Britain.

17   W E McKinlay of the New Zealand forces explains that '…it was not until after the Somme stunt, later in 1916, that the New Zealanders got the name of "The Diggers," which was conferred on them after the Maori Pioneer Battalion had beaten all records in digging the lengthy Turk trench in very fast time. I did not hear the term applied to the Australians until much later in 1917, they being known to everyone in France as the "Aussies"'. (Ernest McKinlay, Late No. 3/1741, N.Z.E.F. http://www.nzetc.org/tm/scholarly/tei-McKWays-t1-body-d2.html)

The dashing soldier in his uniform commanded such universal adulation that Will could not help but unfavourably compare his own humble situation with that of his younger brother. Probably, when he witnessed his family—particularly Dad—gazing upon Charles with boundless pride, he longed for that same regard to be bestowed on him.

It is easy to conjecture that it was this visit by Charles that fired Will's imagination and awoke the first glimmerings of his decision to enlist.

1915: The Bugles of England | 2: The Call to Arms

The bugles of England were blowing o'er the sea,

As they had called a thousand years, calling now to me;

They woke me from dreaming in the dawning of the day,

The bugles of England—and how could I stay?

The banners of England, unfurled across the sea,

Floating out upon the wind were beckoning to me;

Storm-rent and battle-torn, smoke-stained and grey,

The banners of England—and how could I stay?

O England, I heard the cry of those that died for thee,

Sounding like an organ-voice across the winter sea;

They lived and died for England and gladly went their way,

England, O England — how could I stay?[18]

After ten days' leave Charles had to return to duty. On 30 November he was sent to the military camp in Castlemaine, Victoria, where he would remain until his entrance to Duntroon.

The weather was warming up as Christmas approached. December was the busiest time of year for The Salvation Army, for they went around giving Christmas parties, complete with gifts and music, at children's homes, hostels, jails, the Prison Gate Homes, and the Haven.[19]

The casualties of war were tremendous. The AIF needed more soldiers to replace the thousands who had fallen. Colourful recruiting posters were pasted up in public places: in railway stations and bus shelters, on the sides of buildings, on hoardings. Newspapers and magazines carried recruitment advertisements. Most people believed that all eligible able-bodied men ought to enlist, to 'do their duty' and serve Australia and 'The Empire'.

---

18   'For England' — The bugles of England were blowing o'er the sea, by J. D. Burns, 1915. This appears in: The School Paper for Grades VII and VIII, July no. 189 1915; (p. 82) The Bulletin, 1 June vol. 37 no. 1894 1916; (p. 47) The Sydney Mail, 23 July 1919. By the mid-1920s The School Paper had been the prescribed reading material for 30 years in the State elementary/primary schools of the state of Victoria, Australia.

19   The Haven was a hostel for unmarried mothers—homeless young women who had been expelled by their families.

> **Your Country Needs You!**
>
> **RECRUITS WANTED.**
>
> The Defence Department requires EIGHTY men per day to reinforce Victorians at the War
>
> **Will You Make One of this Number?**
>
> Possibly you believe you are justified in not volunteering. Examine your conscience carefully. Is it a valid reason or an excuse?
>
> **Which is Better?**
>
> To fight and perhaps die as AN AUSTRALIAN,
> or you and yours to live under the heel of
>
> **German Militarism.**
>
> **YOUR COUNTRY CALLS**

Great War recruitment poster calling on men in Victoria, Australia

5 QUESTIONS TO MEN WHO HAVE NOT ENLISTED—

1. IF YOU ARE PHYSICALLY FIT AND BETWEEN 18 AND 44 YEARS OF AGE ARE YOU REALLY SATISFIED WITH WHAT YOU ARE DOING TODAY?

2. DO YOU FEEL QUITE HAPPY AS YOU WALK ALONG THE STREETS AND SEE OTHER MEN WEARING THE KING'S UNIFORM?

3. WHAT WILL YOU SAY IN YEARS TO COME WHEN PEOPLE ASK YOU "WHAT DID YOU DO IN THE GREAT WAR?"

4. WHAT WILL YOU ANSWER WHEN YOUR CHILDREN GROW UP AND SAY "FATHER! WHY WEREN'T YOU A SOLDIER TOO?"

5. WHAT WOULD HAPPEN TO THE EMPIRE IF EVERY MAN STAYED AT HOME?

Will was not the only able-bodied man in Australia aged between eighteen and thirty-five and taller than 5 feet 6 inches who had not joined the army, but the number of male civilians was declining daily. By September 1915, such was the need for more soldiers that requirements had been relaxed. Even men in essential occupations were allowed to enlist—to the detriment of the war effort at home.

Several factors stood in the way of his enlistment at this time, not least the moral dilemma of breaking the Bible's sixth commandment, 'Thou shalt not kill'. He was also subject to the occasional 'bilious headache', a condition that might, these days, be called a 'migraine' and, like his father, he sometimes suffered bouts of abdominal pain. Will might have wondered whether he would pass the AIF's medical examination.

Then there was his family. For two years, when he lived and worked in London, he had yearned desperately to be with them. Enlisting in the Australian Imperial Force meant voyaging half a world away to a far-off war, perhaps never to be reunited in this world.

On 15 December 1915 the Australian Prime Minister, Billy Hughes, sent a letter headed 'The Call to Arms' to all the eligible male civilians in Australia, including Will and his brother Frank.

THE CALL TO ARMS

PRIME MINISTER

15th December 1915

Dear Sir—

The present state of war imperatively demands that the exercise of the full strength of the Empire and its Allies should be put forth. In this way only can speedy victory be achieved and lasting peace secured. If those rights and privileges for which Australian democracy has struggled so long and values dearer than life itself is to be preserved, Prussian military despotism must be crushed once and for all.

The resources of the Allies are more than adequate for this task, but they must be marshalled. To wage this war with less than our full strength is to commit national suicide by slowly bleeding to death.

Our soldiers have done great things in this war. They have carved for Australia a niche in the Temple of the Immortals. Those who have died fell gloriously, but had the number of our forces been doubled many brave lives would have been spared, the Australian armies would long ago have been camping in Constantinople, and the world war would have been practically over.

We must put forth all our strength. The more men Australia sends to the front the less the danger will be to each man. Not only victory but safety belongs to the big battalions.

Australia turns to you for help. We want more men. Fifty thousand (50,000) additional troops are to be raised to form new units of the Expeditionary Forces. Sixteen thousand (16,000) men are required each month for reinforcements at the front.

This Australia of ours, the freest and best country on God's earth, calls to her sons for aid. Destiny has given to you a great opportunity. Now is the hour when you can strike a blow on her behalf. If you love your country, if you love freedom, then take your place alongside your fellow-Australians at the front and help them to achieve a speedy and glorious victory.

On behalf of the Commonwealth Government and in the name of the people of Australia I ask you to answer 'Yes' to this appeal, and to do your part in this greatest war of all time.

Yours truly,

W.M. Hughes

PRIME MINISTER OF AUSTRALIA

Will had been born and raised in the quasi-military milieu of The Salvation Army. Even the Army's motto—'Blood and Fire'—evoked battlefield images. Furthermore, as a schoolboy in South Africa, Will had experienced some military training as a member of the Transvaal Scottish Cadets, for four years. Could it be that for him, the call of a military career was becoming quite strong?

He was torn between staying with his beloved family, and donning that striking uniform worn by Charles, with all its associated kudos. Conceivably, the Prime Minister's letter was the last straw that tipped the balance of Will's thinking. At last, after much deliberation, he made his decision.

He would enlist.

Possibly it was significant that Charles had enlisted so soon after he'd heard the news that Will was to join the family in Australia; perhaps it had also been more than coincidence that Will decided to enlist so soon after Charles returned from the front. If sibling rivalry existed between these two, it would not be the first time in history that such a thing had happened.

Perhaps most of all, deep down Will longed for his father to be as proud of him as he was of Charles.

He now faced another difficult decision. His parents, Wiebe and Jacoba, believed in allowing their children to make their own, informed choices in life, but it's likely that Wiebe, for all his pride in Charles's enterprise and advancement, was not entirely happy with his soldier son's choice of career.

The Salvation Army had always encouraged its members to 'express a Christian response to human needs'. They were to show love to their neighbours by 'feeding the hungry, clothing the cold and showing concern for those in need'. For Salvationists it was easier to reconcile these philosophies with joining the armed forces if they chose non-combatant roles such as a the job of musician in a battalion band (bandsmen were also trained as stretcher-bearers), padre (chaplain), which involved administering to the spirit, or that of medical officer (MO), which involved caring for the sick and wounded.

Not all Salvationists felt the same way—Will's brother Charles, for example.

If Will became an infantryman, like Charles, he might risk Dad's tacit disappointment. If he took up a non-combatant role, on the other hand, he could please Dad and Mother while simultaneously stepping into the limelight beside Charlie. The choice seemed clear, but which non-combatant role should he take?

Will knew himself well enough to be certain he would not make a good padre, nor—though he was a good musician and played the cornet in a couple of Salvation Army bands—did he want to become a bandsman.

The first person with whom Will discussed these issues would have been his closest confidante, his father. Whether it was Will himself or 'Colonel' Palstra who suggested he join the Army Medical Corps (AMC) as a medical officer, we cannot know. The letters and diaries merely indicate that it was Will's intention to follow that path after he had enlisted. Once trained as a soldier, he would be eligible to apply for the AMC.

Did he have niggling doubts about this new-found purpose? It did have certain drawbacks. If a man joined the AMC as a medical officer he would, be sent to the battle front, and therefore find himself in as much danger as everyone else, except without a weapon with which to defend himself. It was perilous work—bullets and shells could strike anyone, combatant or not—but M.O.s were saving men's lives, instead of trying to destroy them. Neither medical officers nor men of the Field Ambulance carried any weapons or ammunition. (They still had to learn how to use a gun, just in case).

Men in support roles, such as stretcher-bearers and Field Ambulance, faced as much risk and physical hard work as any infantryman, and they deserved equal kudos. Nevertheless, the newspapers portrayed fighting men as possessing the most glamour and dash, and the public tended to hail them as the heroes.

Perhaps, in the secret recesses of his heart, Will worried about this. Nonetheless, his decision was made.

When he told his parents he was going to enlist, they must have felt quite apprehensive, though they would never show it. Their eldest son assured them that he had no intention of joining up before Christmas—indeed, not before the new year. Maybe Wiebe and Jacoba comforted each other with the thought that there would be several months of training ahead of him before he departed for the battle fronts on the other side of the world, and prayed that by the time he was ready for active service, the war might be over.

Indeed, by December 1915 it was commonly held that the Allies would soon be triumphant.

Christmas Day 1915 was at hand when Australia and New Zealand exploded with jubilation. The Anzacs had finally been evacuated from Gallipoli! Astonishingly, the entire force had withdrawn without casualty. The retreat had taken place in utmost secrecy, so that by 20th December 1915 it was complete, unnoticed by the Turks who continued to bombard the empty trenches.[20] The newspapers were hailing the operation as a 'miracle'.

The ANZAC Corps would now be broken up; the Australian 4th Brigade would be moved to the newly formed Australian 4th Division while New Zealand would form their own unit, the New Zealand Division.

Though it would no longer officially exist, the ANZAC Corps would live on in legend, an integral part of Australian and New Zealand history.

---

20   When winter arrived in November, men froze at their posts and over 16,000 troops with frostbite and exposure were evacuated. It was decided that the campaign could not meet its objectives and the British Empire forces on Gallipoli should withdraw [Evacuation from Gallipoli 1915 | Anzac Portal. anzacportal.dva.gov.au] The troops from Gallipoli were taken first to Lemnos and later to Egypt to await their next assignment.

Part III
1916: To Arms! is the Call

1916: To arms! is the call | 1: Enlistment

God's trumpet is sounding: To arms! is the call;

More warriors are wanted to help in the war;

My King's in the battle, he's calling for me,

A Salvation Soldier for Jesus I'll be.

Stand like the brave! Stand like the brave!

Stand like the brave, with thy face to the foe [21]

On Monday 3 January, 1916, at eleven o'clock in the morning, Will presented himself at the Melbourne Town Hall Recruiting Depot and enlisted in the Australian Imperial Force.

---

21   God's trumpet is sounding. William J Pearson (1832-92) (verses). Fanny Crosby (1820-1915) (chorus)

The entries in Will's pocket diary at the time of his enlistment indicate that he was in a state of joyful expectation and excitement. There is no hint of any reluctance or fear—quite the contrary. He seems to be bubbling over with excited joviality, confident that he would escape harm, and thrilled by the prospect of this utterly new, adventurous career. Indeed, it was a common attitude among those who enlisted, to believe that they would come through the war unscathed.

Diary: my experiences in the A.I.F.

Mon. Jan 3rd, 1916

Presented myself at the Melbourne Town Hall Recruiting Depot at 11am. today (Boxing Day).

On entering the low roofed Town Hall basement doing duty as Recruiting & Attestation Depot, found a large and motley array of men seated on benches placed in rows. A great number seemed rather young—17 years or thereabouts. [Many lads lied about their age in their eagerness to join up.]

At the further end of the basement seated behind a trestle table, were a number of Recruiting Sergeants. The new comer went up to the table where a Sergeant entered up a few preliminary particulars on an Attestation Form [name, date of birth and address]. The applicant then joined himself to the waiting galaxy on the benches, and—waited, not for 10 minutes or even half an hour, but for two solid hours.

In time a Sergeant called out my name, and I sat myself down on a front bench specially provided for those whose period of waiting was destined to terminate soon. Another couple of minutes and the selected number were ushered into a room where the further business of accepting and examining was to be gone through.

We stripped and were measured height and chest, weighed and particulars of colour of hair and eyes taken. Those not coming up to the required height (5' 3") [five foot three inches; the height requirement had been lowered since the beginning of the war] and chest measurement (32' - 34") standard were disqualified at this stage. A sleek and beefy looking Corporal did the measuring and sang out the particulars in a graveyard voice.

The next was a walk [by the hopeful recruits] across the room to the Doctors—wrapped in thought, but nothing more visibly opaque. The men were formed up in batches of from 3 to 8 and a Doctor went down the row examining and testing. A great number of the rejects were for varicose veins and bad teeth. The last test was for eyesight— reading with one eye at a time rows of letters placed at a distance of about 20 feet.

This [final medical test] successfully passed, the men, amongst whom myself, were declared medically fit and could dress. Clerks now completed the attestation papers, whereafter the Swearing in.

Holding a Bible in my right hand I promised "To serve His Majesty George V in the Australian Imperial Force for the period of the War and for 4 months afterwards. To resist the King's enemies and promote the King's peace."

I left the Depot somewhat wearied of waiting and ravenously hungry— dropped into the nearest Restaurant [sic] and appeased the inner man [with a good meal]. Went to Bourke Street ['Colonel' Wiebe Palstra's office at Salvation Army's headquarters] and told Dad.

Private William Palstra was now enlisted in the Australian Imperial Force. Now, there could be no going back.

AUSTRALIAN MILITARY FORCES.
AUSTRALIAN IMPERIAL FORCE.

Attestation Paper of Persons Enlisted for Service Abroad.

No. 555 Name PALSTRA William
V 18408 Unit B. 39th Battalion, A.I.F.
Joined on 3.1.16

Questions to be put to the Person Enlisting before Attestation.

1. What is your Name? — 1. William Palstra
2. In or near what Parish or Town were you born? — 2. In the Parish of Zwolle in or near the Town of Holland in the County of
3. Are you a natural born British Subject or a Naturalized British Subject? (N.B.—If the latter, papers to be shown.) — 3. Natural Born British Subject, Parents British
4. What is your Age? — 4. 24 yrs 2 mths
5. What is your Trade or Calling? — 5. Clerk
6. Are you, or have you been, an Apprentice? If so, where, to whom, and for what period? — 6. No
7. Are you married? — 7. No
8. Who is your next of kin? (Address to be stated) — 8. Father, Col Palstra, 69 Bourke St, Melbourne
9. Have you ever been convicted by the Civil Power? — 9. No
10. Have you ever been discharged from any part of His Majesty's Forces, with Ignominy, or as Incorrigible and Worthless, or on account of Conviction of Felony, or of a Sentence of Penal Servitude, or have you been dismissed with Disgrace from the Navy? — 10. No
11. Do you now belong to, or have you ever served in, His Majesty's Army, the Marines, the Militia, the Militia Reserve, the Territorial Force, Royal Navy, or Colonial Forces? If so, state which, and if not now serving, state cause of discharge — 11. Yes. Transvaal Scottish Cadets 4 yrs
12. Have you stated the whole, if any, of your previous service? — 12. Yes
13. Have you ever been rejected as unfit for His Majesty's Service? If so, on what grounds? — 13. No
14. (For married men, widowers with children, and soldiers who are the sole support of widowed mothers.) Do you understand that no separation allowance will be issued in respect of your service beyond an amount which together with pay would reach eight shillings per day? — 14. —
15. Are you prepared to undergo inoculation against small pox and enteric fever? — 15. Yes

I, William Palstra, do solemnly declare that the above answers made by me to the above questions are true, and I am willing and hereby voluntarily agree to serve in the Military Forces of the Commonwealth of Australia within or beyond the limits of the Commonwealth.

Date 3/1/16

W Palstra
Signature of person enlisted.

WILL PALSTRA'S ENLISTMENT PAPERS

Though Will had signed up, he would not need to depart for the training camp until the end of February. The Pianola Company required a month's notice, and after he left their employ, he spent his last ten days of civilian life on a holiday, accompanying his father on a tour of Tasmania that was part of his Salvation Army work.

From Will's diary on the day he began military service in 1916:

> Tuesday Feb 29th
>
> Presented myself at Sturt Street, Melbourne at 8.45 a.m. as per instructions. Medical inspection, and a rather hurried lunch provided by the Ladies' Patriotic Committee.

Imagine a motley assortment of young men clad in the attire of their various callings, from dungarees (overalls) or trousers held up by braces, to Edwardian three-piece 'sack' suits and high-collared shirts with neckties; with head-wear from baggy tweed caps to derbies or bowler hats, and foot-wear from sturdy boots to polished oxford shoes. Will owned very few clothes. We know he had a Salvation Army uniform, a suit he wore at the office, and probably a long overcoat, but what other garments he possessed is a matter for conjecture.

After lunch the rag-tag bunch of recruits, headed by a brass military band, marched through the city streets to the cheers of enthusiastic onlookers.

At Spencer Street Station a locomotive waited by the platform, a pillar of dense black smoke pouring from its smokestack and blowing away across the rail yards. The crowd of recruits poured into the carriages, cramming themselves into the wood-panelled compartments. Doors banged, boots crunched across floors. They tossed their bags up onto overhead wire racks supported by ornate brass brackets.

'All aboard!' the station-master was shouting. He stood on the platform glancing up and down the row of carriages. 'Stand clear!'

The guard blew his whistle and the locomotive let out a slow, mournful shriek. Hissing jets of steam spurted from between its iron wheels. Snorting and chugging amidst a swirl of vapours, the train pulled out, gradually gathering speed. Soon it had left the station far behind.

It was heading for a large and beautiful rural city, the second most important settlement in Victoria. The 19th-century gold rush had changed Ballarat from a small sheep station to a major settlement. The city was renowned for its wide boulevards, magnificent Victorian-era architecture, huge collection of public statuary and grand public gardens.

Ballarat Railway Station, early 20th century

It was here that the recruits ended their railway journey and marched through the streets to the training camp, a twelve-acre site abutting the north-east shore of Lake Wendouree.

Private William Palstra's war diary, Tuesday 29 February 1916:

March through Ballarat streets headed by Band. Chaps cheer us lustily as we enter the Show Grounds Camp beside Lake Wendouree. Medical inspection. Blankets, plates, spoons and forks issued, and quartered in old sheep pens, open at one side and ventilated on all sides...

To the shock and indignation of the recruits, their quarters turned out to be the showgrounds' sheep pens. In these most rudimentary of shelters, roofed with corrugated iron, draughty, uncomfortable and completely lacking in privacy, they had to sleep on straw mattresses. That night was chilly, Ballarat being notorious for its unpredictable and extreme weather.

'Corner of the Camp', Ballarat 1916

1916: To arms! is the call | 2: Ballarat Training Camp

The Mother call'd, and they heard, | Her children over the foam;

The Mother spake but a word, | And the word that she spake was "Home!"

And they answer'd, "Mother, we come !" | And, swift as the homing bird

Gathers wheeling in autumn skies, | High hearts uplifted and stirr'd,

They rose, as the hurricanes rise,| With a lightning of clarion replies.

With the armour of freedom they gird, | Them to war: from Canadian snows,

Out of uttermost Ind, and a third |Where the Austral acacia blows

They muster to smite her foes. | Thro' the thunder of oceans they came:

They sprang to her bugle's call |Young warriors who sought not fame,

But only to render their all | For the Homeland; to fight and to fall.[22]

22　'The Mother and her Sons' by Charles Edward Byles, March, 1916

William Palstra's war diary, Wednesday 1 March 1916:

> Spent a fairly comfortable night on my palliasse of straw. Very cold in morning. Reveille 6 a.m. Bugles play the "Rouse" and Band follows up with a tune. A mug of hot coffee and "jerks" ["physical jerks", ie. exercises].
>
> Initiated during the day into the mysteries of squad drill in single rank without arms. Issued with blueys, kit bag, underclothing etc. Clothing very good, best wool, good finish. Find I am in "B" Coy, 39th Batt.

In 1916 the Australian Imperial Force, the main expeditionary force of the Australian Army, was a corps comprising five infantry divisions and two light horse divisions. Will's battalion, the 3th, was part of the newly-formed Third Division.

A division comprised three brigades, while a brigade was composed of four battalions. It was the battalions with which the men would come to most strongly identify, as a brotherhood-in-arms.

Each battalion was divided into four companies, which in turn were split into four platoons. Lieutenants (or Second Lieutenants) were the leaders of platoons, which were divided into four sections, each made up of a corporal, a lance corporal and eight privates. The section was considered the 'building block' of the army. It was the smallest fighting unit.

Later, looking back on these first few days in camp, Will would write:

> Of my training there little need be said except a reference to two matters which had some considerable influence on my future as a soldier. The first of these is that I found myself housed in a sheep pen in the Show-Grounds, and that my stable companions were drovers and labourers whose manner of life had up to that point been a closed book to me. The book was soon opened. In it I read not only much about myself hitherto unsuspected, but also much which proved of great value to me later...

Will's introduction to army life was an awakening in many ways. He had led a relatively sheltered life within the circle of The Salvation Army. Now, he took a delighted interest in his new comrades.

They had come together from all over Victoria, some riding hundreds of miles from remote country towns and isolated farms in the bush or the desert, others from the cities and the suburbs, from factories, offices and universities to join what they viewed as a thrilling and dangerous undertaking, and a noble cause. They were drovers and labourers, painters and hotel managers, grocers, farmers, butchers, dairymen, bricklayers, seamen, miners, printers, drapers, hatters, tram conductors, shearers, carpenters, horse drivers and policemen. Most were men whose way of life had, up to that point, been beyond the bounds of Will's experience. The single thing they all now had in common was the army.

With a lively sense of fun they skylarked and played pranks whenever they felt they could get away with them; for example, conducting night raids on the tents of other companies. They belched, swore, smoked, whistled, sang, wrestled, bantered and indulged in horseplay, and laughed easily. Most had no respect whatsoever for authority unless that authority had proved itself to them. As for obeying orders—most of the men had never, in adulthood, been subject to a direct command. They complied—usually—despite being somewhat affronted. Generally, they scorned officers. They were vigorously averse to saluting them or calling them 'sir', unless the officer had earned their regard.

To Will, encountering such a rich medley of characters and backgrounds must have seemed like entering another world. In the course of his work for The Salvation Army he had met people from many walks of life, but he had never lived so intimately amongst men who worked on the land. Theirs was an outlook that contrasted starkly with the attitudes to which he had become accustomed.

In Salvation Army circles, for example, people never swore or took the name of the Lord in vain. They never smoked or gambled. Neither did Salvationists publicly proclaim that they longed for a cold beer; indeed, they never touched alcohol at all, unless it were to be used as cleaning fluid.

These men valued courage and scorned cowardice whenever they suspected it. Slang expressions which they'd picked up from other soldiers, or from their various trades, enlivened their language. Frequently they referred to the AIF as the 'Ack I Foof'. Men who quailed were called 'windy' or 'ringers'. Complainers were called 'grousers' or 'whingers'. They loathed malingerers, calling them 'lead-swingers', scorned sycophants, whom they called 'scales'—because one had to have scales on one's belly to be a crawler—and hated 'polers'; men who, like the pair of bullocks nearest to the pole of the wagon, did less than their share of work, thereby rendering the other fellow's task more difficult. 'Spring-heel' was their term for a man who, on joining a fighting unit had second thoughts and immediately found a means to leave it.

All the newcomers were impatient to obtain their khakis and accoutrements. Uniforms were a powerful drawcard in recruiting; young men were frequently attracted to the army after seeing a regiment of well-drilled warriors march down the street magnificently attired in their dashing outfits, rifles angled over their shoulders and bayonets flashing. It was commonly bruited, too, that women were attracted to uniformed men. After enlisting, most young men could hardly wait to go home wearing their khaki, to impress their families and the ladies.

Nevertheless, the recruits had to wait. On that first day they were issued with 'blueys'—[23] the training camp uniform consisting of blue dungarees—in addition to all the necessities of life as a trainee soldier. The complete list included a hat badge, a universal kit bag, a pair of ankle boots with laces, a pair of braces, a hair brush, a shaving brush, a tooth brush, a comb, two pairs of drawers, a fork, a greatcoat, a khaki felt hat, a white hat, a hold-all, a cardigan jacket, a dungaree jacket, a dinner knife, a razor and case, two flannel shirts, two singlets, three pairs of woollen socks, a spoon, a chin strap, two towels, two pairs of dungaree trousers, a cake of soap and two 'abdominal belts'. There was also a 'pocket housewife'—pronounced 'hussif'—a

---

23   Some AIF units were issued with dungarees, some with older versions of khaki uniforms from pre-war days, others with yellow/tan cotton clothing. The full khaki issue came later, as available. Source: Ted Harris.

roll of khaki drill cloth about ten inches (250mm) long and four inches (100mm) wide, lined with flannelette containing needles, thread, buttons and other sewing accoutrements, all rolled up and secured with tape.

There were no pyjamas in the new kit. The men would have to sleep in their underwear.

The men's civilian clothes were taken away—later, when the men went on leave, these bundles would be returned to them so that they could carry them back to their families. Among the recruits there was a sense of exhilaration at receiving their new outfits, even though they had been told they would not be issued with their proper khaki uniforms and web equipment until closer to the time of embarkation. Spirits rose high, and witty—sometimes coarse—repartee flew back and forth.

Mingling with the irreverent, high-spirited, self-confident and somewhat lawless men of the 39th Battalion at the Ballarat Training Camp, Will experienced a kind of culture shock, and he seems to have found a new self-awareness. He was attracted to the active, exciting way of life that a combat role offered. It was a life unbounded by the walls of an office, a life led beneath open skies.

This mild-mannered, dutiful office-clerk was beginning to feel the unfolding of an inner confidence he'd not known before. This was borne out on Thursday March 2nd 1916, the second day of training, which would turn out to be a pivotal point in his life.

It began much in the manner of the first. The brass band, at full volume, marched through the tent lines immediately after the bugler sounded reveille to get the men out of bed. The recruits—enlivened by hot coffee, physical jerks and breakfast—assembled on the parade ground for squad drill. Standing in front of the rows of dungaree-clad men, an officer loudly called out, 'Anyone who has previous military experience should step out and be tried out for the rank of non-commissioned officer.'

The idea of being promoted to NCO appealed to many of the recruits for a number of reasons, not least because higher ranks enjoyed more privileges and their pay was better than the private soldier's allotment of five shillings a day. Perhaps it also appealed to Private

Palstra because he had once held the rank of 'captain' in The Salvation Army, because he wanted to make Dad proud, and because his younger brother Charles was already an officer.

Nonetheless he was aware that, as he later wrote, 'his military experience, to all intents and purposes, was nil', consisting of some drills of doubtful value learned as a corporal in the tartan-uniformed Transvaal Scottish Cadets during his high school days at Johannesburg in South Africa, and some tips he had picked up the previous day. He felt reluctant to put himself forward.

Glancing in the direction of those who did, however, he noticed that some of them were men who—he had learned from conversing with them on the previous day—could know little more than he did. His amazement was followed quickly by the realisation that here was, perhaps, an opportunity. And so he stepped forward, feeling that the worst that could happen to him was to be unceremoniously ordered back to the ranks.

To each of those men who had presented themselves, the platoon commander allotted a squad of eight men. Will marched his squad off successfully—a good distance away from inquisitive eyes. Having put the men through a couple of simple movements he remembered from cadets, he told them they were doing splendidly, stood them at ease, and had a good look around to see what the other would-be NCOs were doing, so that he could mimic them.

By repeating these tactics he managed to get through the day.

That evening, Private Palstra walked to the shop in the camp and bought the small army-issue booklet entitled 'Infantry Training 1914'. By dint of serious attention to the contents during off-duty hours, and what he felt was 'considerable luck' during the first few days, the depth of his ignorance remained undiscovered.

In his pocket diary he wrote:

> Thurs. 2/3/16. Appointed instructor on strength of having been a Corporal in Transvaal Cadets, and drill Squad all day, on the system of combining what I learned yesterday with what I see others doing. Shuffle along with considerable success. Buy Inf. Training Book.

Part IV
1916: Where Are Our Uniforms?

1916: Where Are Our Uniforms? | 1: A Temporary Corporal

"Where are our uniforms?

Far, far, away.

When will our rifles come?

P'raps, p'raps some day.

All we need is just a gun

For to chase the bloody Hun.

Think of us when we are gone,

Far, far away."[24]

---

24   "Where are our Uniforms?" was sung by World War I soldiers to the tune "There Is A Happy Land Far, Far Away". Author unknown.

The allied nations foresaw that 1916 would be a crucial year. They had come to realise that early hopes of a speedy victory in the Great War must be replaced by a determination to fight a long and bitter campaign, right to the finish.

As part of this effort, the Australian government decided to form new AIF infantry divisions. The Fourth and Fifth Infantry Divisions began forming from seasoned fighting men of the First and Second Divisions in Egypt in February 1916. The Third Division was to be formed from new recruits in Australia, in March. Will and his comrades of the 39th Battalion at the Ballarat camp were destined to be part of it.

Many men of the new Third Division felt uncomfortable to think that their unit appeared to have been given naming precedence over the seasoned fighting-men, when they had done nothing as yet to prove their valour. They had no say in it, however.

Soldiers of the older divisions would soon nickname the Third Division 'the baby division'[25] because it was the last to go into action.

Nicknames were popular. At Gallipoli and for a short time afterwards, the 'Old Kangaroos' had derogatorily referred to men who had failed to enlist by 1915 as 'Deep Thinkers', because they took so long to think about joining. Eventually this was replaced by the term 'Fair Dinkums' when the Old Kangaroos realized that anyone who joined the army after reading the casualty lists from Gallipoli and the early battles in France and Flanders must be 'fair dinkum' (genuine).

Nevertheless, in revenge for the slur on their manhood, some of the new recruits derided the early AIF volunteers of 1914 as 'Tourists'. The term was short for 'five bob[26] a day tourists', because it was alleged that they had expected the war to end before they could be fit to take the field, and therefore enlisted merely for the pay and opportunity to travel. These cynics were few and soon howled down.

---

25   Source: www.diggerhistory.info

26   A 'bob' is slang for a 'shilling.'

Will Palstra's war diary: Monday 6 March 1916:

> Commence training in the "Gardens" by the side of Lake Wendouree. Get blistered feet. Put up tents in afternoon and move quarters to these.

Will's accent must have appeared rather 'upper class English' to the men among whom he found himself. Due to the British Empire's global transcendence at that time, this would have lent him some authority. He would not, however, have been alone—many of the other recruits were British-born.

English accents were highly esteemed in the antipodes. It was important, however, not to sound too 'upper-crust'. There was a fine distinction between an English accent and a pompous way of speaking. Generally, AIF soldiers scorned officers whose accent they considered 'too jammy'. According to war journalist CW Bean, they would tolerate a wide range of behaviours, but drew the line at anything that they thought of as affectation.

As a section commander Will was classified as a 'temporary corporal', a rank that could be stripped from him at a moment's notice. He felt a fierce urge to increase his status to 'corporal', the next rank up from 'private', so he kept a close eye on job vacancies. He was in luck!

> Thursday 9-3-16 At afternoon Parade Clerks, Cooks, Storemen are asked to step out. The job I fancied, C.Q.M.S.[27] proved to be already filled on the principle of first come first served.

> Shorthand typists were also in demand, but although rank and pay of Corporal is attached to these positions I felt the open air life of the Infantry would suit me better. On re-joining my Section Mr Lenton picked me out with 3 others for the N.C.O.'s school. Paraded at 5 pm before the O.C. Captain H.O.A.D. Burrowes, who, on the recommendation of the Platoon Cmr, orders me to attend a Battalion N.C.O.'s School to commence on Monday evening next at 7 pm.

---

27 Company Quartermaster Sergeant

On Friday 17 March Will became an Acting Corporal, which meant that he was now in charge of a quarter of a platoon. The men of his new section, lined up for his inspection, bestowed on him that measuring look he knew so well. He would have to earn their respect.

Why 'Acting Corporal' and not fully-fledged corporal? The big difference was that until his rank was confirmed, his corporal's stripes could be taken away at his commanding officer's whim. After he was 'substantive' he could only lose them if he seriously bungled, and Will was determined not to let that happen.

From Will's diary:

> Thursday 23rd-3-16 Drilled a squad in musketry. Felt shaky on it. Rest in afternoon, tactical march at night.

> Friday 31st-3-16 At Canadian Butts[28] in afternoon 2 hrs trench digging. Phoned to Camp for O.C. from Canadian Home[29] re keeping dinner warm for men. Led the left file of Coy. back to Camp.

Will's diary entry of 31 March records him showing initiative and resourcefulness, and being recognised for it by being given a high-status task. For the first time in his life he headed a column of seventy men along the public roads of a city, and one wonders, as he entered the gates of the camp, whether he managed to keep a suitably serious expression on his face.

---

28 Canadian Butts was a rifle range, so named because Canadian miners had worked diggings there during Ballarat's gold rush, and had left their name all over the place, in 'Canadian lead'—the vein of ore itself—'Canadian Springs', and 'Canadian Creek'. The rifle range was one of many dotted all over the state, originally created for the use of the Victorian Ranger battalions. It had been built in the middle 1800s when the ability to fire a rifle accurately was the mark of a good soldier, and it was now the location where trainee soldiers practised digging trenches and firing rifles and machine guns. They called it 'Canadian Butts'; 'butt' meaning 'target', and not 'buttocks' as it came to mean in the 21st century.

29 Canadian Home is the dwelling of the Range Keeper who lived in a house on the range site.

On the morning of Wednesday 22 March Will's name was read out in Company Orders as having passed Battalion NCO's School. Imagine his joy and triumph as, during the mid-day meal in the mess hall he celebrated with the others who had passed.

Corporal Palstra was being noticed by men further up in the military hierarchy. Not only his accent distinguished him, but also his resourcefulness, his dutiful, unquestioning obedience to authority, and his attitude of uncomplaining self-denial, which he had learned as a member of The Salvation Army. He probably stood in stark contrast to many of his fellow recruits.

Towards the end of March, excitement rippled through the camp when the long-awaited new khaki uniforms and web equipment arrived. Up till then, the recruits had been clothed in dark blue dungarees.

AIF headquarters also provided colour patches and unit badges for the soldiers to sew on to the sleeves of their tunics. The colour patch was a piece of woven cloth, its geometrical shape identifying the formation to which the wearer's unit belonged. The 39th's oval colour patch was brown above and red below—'Mud over Blood' as the men of the battalion came to call the badge; an affectionate term that was, in future days, to prove only too appropriate.

Regimental transport to the 39th Battalion

Acting Corporal Palstra and his NCO comrades unrolled their 'hussifs' and stitched the battalion's elliptical colour patches to the sleeves, about one and a half inches below each shoulder.

The disgruntled privates did not have to wait for long for clothing, patches and badges. Like the NCOs they were soon summoned to one of the marquees to line up and receive their parcels. This was followed by a lecture in the use and purpose of the new apparel, particularly the web equipment.

According to the Digger History website's information about webbing:

'The Pattern 1908 Web Equipment was designed so that the complete set, which was called the 'Marching Order' equipment, could be divided into two parts. The first part consisted of the holders necessary for the carrying of a rifle with sling, a bayonet, ammunition, an entrenching tool, a water bottle and a haversack. To these could be added one 'iron ration', a knife, a spoon, a fork and as much extra food as may be accommodated in the haversack. If required, the first portion could be worn on its own. It was known as 'battle order.'

'The second part comprised the pack and supporting straps, which could easily be removed from the first portion of the equipment. Together with the contents of the pack, it could be discarded if necessary, or added if the opportunity arose. The pack contained a greatcoat, a 'comforter' cap, a spare pair of socks, a mess tin and cover, a tooth brush, a shaving brush and hold-all, a razor, comb, towel, soap and a housewife. This arrangement allowed the soldier to keep all his equipment with him while, if necessity demanded, the pack could be discarded and extra ammunition in cotton bandoliers carried in its place. The whole web could be removed from the body with one movement, and unless it was required to be taken apart for any purpose, it remained intact and ready for putting on again at short notice.

'The advantages of such an arrangement were obvious. First of all, men could turn out in barracks or camp fully equipped in a few moments, even in the dark. Separate articles had not to be hunted for, by no means an easy matter in a crowded tent; all that each man had to do was to seize his rifle and equipment and double to the place of assembly, and within a few seconds of his arrival he would be ready to march off. Again, when a halt occurred on the line of march, every man could at once, if he wished, divest himself of the whole of his load, resuming it the moment the order was given to fall in.

'Secondly, the equipment was perfectly balanced. All former equipments had suffered from the defect that with no ammunition in the pouches in front, and with a pack or rolled great coat on the back, the weight of the latter pulled up the belt in front.

'Thirdly, there were no straps crossing the chest. This feature, taken in conjunction with the second, accounted for the fact, that the soldier could at all times march with his waist belt undone, and every button of his coat unfastened. During manoeuvres and in the field no restriction should be placed upon this being done unless an order to the contrary be specially given. The advantages to be derived there-from were too obvious to mention, but it should be clearly understood that the correct balance of the equipment is in no way impaired even under these conditions.

'Finally, note the flexibility of the equipment. With the exception of the pack which, when worn, must always be to the back, the articles carried by the soldier can be disposed in a variety of ways. By means of the end pieces provided there are altogether four places in which the haversack, water bottle, and entrenching tool can be carried, and their relative positions can therefore be varied at will. For example, assuming the pack to have been discarded, the haversack and water bottle can be taken away from their normal positions on the hips, fastened together, and placed on the back. In this way the hips are freed from everything except the bayonet and entrenching tool, whereby the man's actions are less hampered, especially in rough or difficult country.' [30]

The recruits each received three hats as standard issue; a peaked cap, a field cap and a distinctively Australian slouch hat.

---

30   The 1908 Pattern Infantry Web Equipment (webbing). www.diggerhistory.info/pages-equip/web-1908.htm

1916: Where are our uniforms? | 2: A Decision is Made

The Ballarat Courier Friday 3 March 1916 page 4

```
A BATTALION MASCOT.

Nearly all of the brigades and battalions which have left
our shores for the front have had a mascot of one kind or
another — dogs, kangaroos, or animals of some kind. The 39th
Battalion, which will bear the name of our city, Ballarat,
is not yet possessed of a mascot. A gift of a well-bred
fox terrier or bull pup would be much appreciated. If one
is available the secretary of the citizens' committee (Mr.
T. Harris) would be pleased to hear from the donor, whose
kindly act will be acknowledged.
```

Note: The battalion was given a bulldog as their mascot.

Will had formed a friendship with the Reverend Joyce of the Ballarat Congregational church, who invited him to tea at the grand old manse in Mair Street. The conversation turned to music, and when Joyce found out that Will enjoyed singing, he asked if he would like to lead the congregation in prayer and sing a hymn at the evening service.

The church was a masterpiece of ornate Victorian architecture. Inside, at the far end of the nave, a great fence of ornate organ pipes, thirty feet high, stood like slender ivory sentinels above the wood panels backing the keyboard.

Every Sunday night the place was packed from wall to wall with worshippers.

After the Reverend Joyce's introduction, Will rose to his feet and took his place on a low dais facing the assembly. First he led them in prayer for the fallen, the injured and for those who were away fighting.

The hymn, poignantly, was entitled, 'When the Roll is Called.' The organist played a few preliminary bars and Will took a deep breath.

'When the trumpet of the Lord shall sound and time shall be no more,

And the morning breaks, eternal, bright and fair:

When the saved of earth shall gather over on the other shore,

And the roll is called up yonder, I'll be there.'

Those who watched him as he stood alone lifting up his voice, the golden light of the overhead lamps falling softly on his young face and neat uniform, must have been moved. Most people had family members who had departed on active service, many of whom would never return to their homeland. The organist played softly, saving the full power of the instrument for the swelling chorus.

'When the roll is called up yonder,

When the roll is called up yonder,

When the roll is called up yonder,

When the roll is called up yonder, I'll be there.

The music echoed thrilllingly from the vaulted ceiling and charged the air. It can be imagined that as the deep, bone-shaking notes boomed out, an unbearable longing and profound sense of loss must have surged in the hearts of the listeners. Will sang on in his clear strong voice, though there was scarcely a dry eye to be seen among those who crowded the pews.

From Will's Diary:

> Sunday 26-3-16 Had a walk round the Lake with Allan Fisher in the afternoon. Tea with the Rev. Joyce, Congregational Minister at the Parsonage, Mair Street, at 5 p.m. Took part in Service in the evening. Prayed and soloed — "When the Roll is called."

BALLARAT CONGREGATIONAL CHURCH 1916

Early in March, Will had submitted the application forms to join the AMC. By the end of the first month's infantry training, however, his quandary about whether to become a medical officer had resolved itself.

He was not the right material for the Medical Corps, of this he was now certain. The more he thought about the life of a medical officer the less it appealed to him. He was not the kind of man to relish having to clean and bandage festering wounds, or hold down a screaming, struggling patient while a gangrenous or shattered limb was amputated.

The life of an infantryman, on the other hand, had made Will feel more alive and more self-assured than he had ever thought possible. He was better suited for that role. His aptitude, he believed, lay in leadership and action, not rescuing and medicine.

Will had been a Salvation Soldier all his life, fighting to save souls, fighting for ideals, and in a curious way the AIF must have seemed like a logical extension of all that had gone before. Bellowing choruses of 'blood and fire' he had gone into battle for The Salvation Army. With blood and deadly gunfire he would now fight for his country.

Yes, he would remain in the infantry. It was decided. It was done. He told his parents and they accepted his decision with equanimity.

Part V
1916: Dash and Determination

1916: Dash and Determination | 1: Preparing to Depart

This Day of Days shall sacred be,

In truth—a loving memory

Of those who fought, of those who died,

Australia's and New Zealand's pride.[31]

On Wednesday 19 April Ballarat seethed with excitement. After the months of training and speculation, the 39th had received word that they would embark for active service on 27 May. The men responded with delight to the news.

AIF Headquarters had requisitioned special trains to transport soldiers to Melbourne on leave, that very Wednesday night. 'Final leave' was to extend over Easter until Anzac Day.

---

31   Ode to Anzac Day, April 25th, 1915. Dedicated and presented to 'The Anzacs' by the author, in memory of his son Allan Begbie Campbell, of the 12th ALH Regiment, killed in action near Gaza, on the 19th of April, 1917.

Crowded with high-spirited men, the trains from Ballarat pulled into Spencer Street Station that evening under the glare of electric lighting. The passengers spilled forth in a laughing, whooping, exuberant tide. Will wasted no time in legging it to Flinders Street and catching a late suburban train to Westgarth Station.

Six days' leave before those last few weeks in Ballarat! There was much to do in Melbourne, numerous people to see, many farewells to make, in addition to all the usual duties of a Salvationist family over the period of Easter.

It was customary for soldiers who were about to embark on active service to have their photographs professionally taken. This image would be a memento for the family to treasure; especially important given that many of the fresh-faced young men whose eyes seemed filled with calm optimism as they gazed out of those soft, sepia portraits would never return home. The studio photograph, though fairly costly, might in some cases end up being the only record by which a family could remember their son; their brave soldier proudly wearing his uniform.

Dad had booked an appointment for Will at Alpha Photographic Studios in the city, so next day he was back on the train again, heading for central Melbourne.

For this sitting, Corporal Palstra decided to wear the British-looking peaked cap. Most of his comrades wore the same hat for their photographs. These men were about to put their lives at risk for the British Empire, and no doubt they wanted to look as British as possible.

At Alpha Studios, wearing his peaked cap and army greatcoat, Will seated himself on a chair in front of a painted canvas which could be pulled down to cover the wall and pulled up again like a window blind if a different scenic background was required. The photographer told him to remain very still. In silence—except for the click of the camera shutter and the low rumble of traffic outside the window—the photograph was taken. Will's image, the face of a calm young man gazing meditatively into the distance, or into the future—was burned forever into a dusting of silver on the photographic plate.

Back at home, in a private moment, Will's parents presented him with a small golden locket on a chain. Picture him accepting the gift from his mother's hands, unwrapping the small parcel and gazing at the contents with undisguised pleasure. No doubt his parents, delighting in his expression of gratitude, urged him to open it on the spot.

Will presses the clasp and the locket swings open on its hinges. Within each of the two compartments nestled a photograph; Mother on one side, Father on the other, wearing their Salvation Army uniforms. After gazing at the images for a while Will says 'Thank you,' and carefully closes the case. The lump in his throat prevents him from saying more. The cost of the ornament would have made a significant inroad into his parents' meagre savings, but they had not stinted.

His mother, knowing nothing about military life, tells him she is making a small mattress for him to take overseas.

'No need, Mum!' Will probably assures her. 'The AIF supplies everything.'

'But I am sure the army mattresses will not be at all comfortable,' says Mother, 'and you must get your sleep!'

It's her way of sending a little part of herself with her child, he knows; her only way of protecting and comforting him when vast gulfs of distance separated them. The larger the quantity of useful hand-made gifts she could send with him when he went away, the happier she would feel. He thanks her with a kiss.

The Sydney Morning Herald, Tuesday 25 April 1916, Page 5
ANZAC

Australia's great heart is throbbing today as it has never throbbed before. For April 25 — "Anzac Day"—is a day that will live in our hearts and in our history as long as Australia lasts. And this is the first anniversary of Anzac Day.

A year and a day ago Australia was just the old Australia, Australians the old Australians, not known greatly to the world outside. We had, it was true, thrown in our lot with the great mother country in the war in which she had suddenly found herself, and we had gathered our men together and sent them abroad to fight for her; and for months — some weary months—they had been camped in the shadow of the Pyramids. . . .

Far off from Australia, in the grey of an April morning, when the dawn was struggling with the last shades of night, Australian and New Zealand soldiers wore storming the frowning heights, of Gallipoli, in the face of it murderous fire. Men were falling by the score, but not one faltered. Many fell, but the rest climbed up the steep slopes— climbed up and up—climbing to a place among the nations. "It seemed an impossible task," it has been written, "but those men performed the impossible" . . .

To-day, as we celebrate the brave deeds of our heroes on Gallipoli, that Immortal landing of April 25, when Australia suddenly emerged to adult nationhood, we also commemorate the death of those who laid down their lives for their country . . .

And we pledge ourselves on this day to comfort the widowed and the fatherless, and to see to it that those who return to us with their wounds upon them will never be forgotten.

. . .'"Whatever the destiny of the Australian people, however long the span of life this nation shall enjoy, however great the achievements of all the future years, the glory of Anzac Day never shall be dimmed. For Australia that day was baptism and regeneration, awakening and fulness of life. In a very high and blessed sense, the men who died at Anzac were the saviours of this people."

They made a new Australia. This is the day we celebrate—commemorate.

Tuesday, the last day of Will's 'final leave', was first anniversary of Anzac Day.[32]

It was twelve months since the Australian and New Zealand Army Corps's landing at Gallipoli. At nine o'clock in the morning people throughout the state of Victoria ceased to labour and shouted, 'Hip, hip, hooray!' for the King, the Empire and the 'Anzacs'. Right across the world, wherever there were Australians or New Zealanders, it was a grand, emotional and spectacular occasion. The day was marked by a wide variety of ceremonies, marches and services throughout Australia and New Zealand, and a sports day in the Australian camp in Egypt. Wounded soldiers from Gallipoli attended the Sydney march in convoys of cars, attended by nurses. In New Zealand more than two thousand people attended the service in Rotorua. In London, there was a service in Westminster Abbey and thousands of Australian and New Zealand troops marched through the streets. An English newspaper headline dubbed them 'The Knights of Gallipoli'.

Australian newspapers eulogised,

> 'The price of nationhood must be paid in blood and tears. Before the Anzacs astonished the watching nations, we were Australian in name, and we had a flag, but generally speaking, it was assumed that Australia only lived by the grace of England. Anzac Day has changed all that and we are at last a nation, with one heart, one soul. There is mourning in our homes and grief in our hearts, and the flower of our youth will not return to us but the spirit of our dead heroes has come home across the seas to whisper that we have taken our place among the nations.'

---

32   On 30 April 1915, when the first news of the landing reached New Zealand, a half-day holiday was declared and impromptu services were held. The following year a public holiday was gazetted (officially declared) on 5 April and services to commemorate were organised by the returned servicemen. Source: 'The Making of Anzac Day', New Zealand History online — Nga korero aipurangi o Aotearoa, History Group, Ministry for Culture and Heritage, Wellington, New Zealand. Accessed 16 June 2007.

And from His Majesty King George V:

> Tell my people of Australia that today I am joining with them in their solemn tribute to the memory of their heroes who died in Gallipoli.
>
> They gave their lives for a supreme cause in gallant comradeship with the rest of my sailors and soldiers who fought and died with them. Their valour and fortitude have shed fresh lustre on the British arms.
>
> May those who mourn their loss find comfort in the conviction that they did not die in vain, but that their sacrifice has drawn our peoples more closely together and added strength and glory to the empire.

The first Anzac Day was a national obsession. The newly coined word 'Anzac' shone with a sort of sacredness. It seemed that the entire population was treating men in khaki like knights, or heroes, or even angels. In the cities and throughout rural areas the day was packed with marching parades, church services, concerts, luncheons and dinners, recruiting rallies and ceremonies. In Victoria it was not just Anzac Day, but officially Anzac Week. Events staged on Anzac Sunday and Anzac Day itself attracted enormous crowds.[33] The public crammed themselves into public squares, parks, town halls and churches. Several newspapers brought out special Anzac Day editions and continued the theme over the full week.

The atmosphere was imbued with a profound sense of mourning. It was like a funeral on a national scale, as if the entire community were grieving.

Australia's entire population—babies, children, women, men, the elderly—numbered only five million. 8,700 Australians in total had died at Gallipoli and now, twelve months afterwards, Australia's sons were still perishing on the battlefields.

---

33   'A Sob Seemed to Shake the Community' by Ian Warden. National Library 14 of Australia News.

Among the dead were 2721 New Zealanders. A large percentage[34] of the male population of both countries had already enlisted, and more were being called for.

The classified sections of the newspapers, on 25 April 1916, were filled with column after column of memorials to the men who had lost their lives a year earlier.

> 'No matter how we pray, dear brother,
>
> No matter how we call;
>
> There's nothing left to answer
>
> But your photo on the wall...'[35]

Grief-stricken parents, wives, children and siblings, clad in the shadowy shades of mourning, were to be seen amongst every gathering and congregation. People made way for them, showing utmost respect. Some glanced towards them with heartfelt sympathy, and quickly glanced away, leaving them privacy for their tears.

> 'No one he loved was by his side
>
> To hear his last faint sigh;
>
> Or whisper just one loving word,
>
> Or even say goodbye...'[36]

---

34   By ANZAC Day 1916 only a small number of AIF units had arrived in France from Egypt.

35   The Benbow family's tribute in *The Age*, 1916, to Mervin, 'our dear son and brother …killed at the Dardanelles'.

36   Eva Brown, in *The Age*, 1916—a tribute to her brother Roy Gardner.

'It is a day,' said one archbishop in his Anzac Day sermon, 'for pride and sorrow, but sorrow has to come first, because we are here first and foremost to mourn our loss. We cannot dwell on it, we cannot contemplate the cutting off of those bright young lives, so rich with varied promise, without wincing with pain.'[37]

The presence of returned servicemen in the congregation forcibly brought home the reality of the tragedy.

'There was hardly one man of the five hundred Anzacs who paraded for the service,' one journalist wrote, 'who did not bear the pathetic marks of wounds or illness. They included sightless men who were led by their comrades; men all hunched and with trembling limbs that could but shuffle along; men on crutches; men with empty sleeves or useless arms,' and almost every face looked haunted, as if not twelve months, not eternity could ever efface the terrible memories of Anzac. 'There were men, too, who had to be carried into the service. They were laid in invalids' chairs at the steps of the chancel beneath the pulpit.'

Despite the intensity of patriotic fervour, the recruiting drives achieved lacklustre results. Even the thrilling spectacle of returned Anzacs marching through the streets failed to boost the numbers of men volunteering for service. Melbourne's *The Age* newspaper forewarned that the low numbers were 'fast sounding the death knell of the voluntary system.' Journalists across the land painted a harrowing picture of a grieving populace, equally crushed by desolation as it was elevated by patriotic pride. On Anzac Day it seemed as if the whole nation was rocked by a convulsion of weeping. On 26 April the newspapers declared, 'Though the record of Anzac is written in gold, the page is yet wet with tears.'[38]

---

37   Brisbane Courier, 6 April 1916

38   Sydney Morning Herald, 1916

1916: Dash and Determination | 2: Marching Through the City

Britain's sons are fighting

That Britain might be free

For pride of race and pride of place

And freedom of the sea.

And our Colonial heroes

Add to her lustrous fame,

And on far off Gallipoli

Achieved a deathless name.

Chorus: A.N.Z.A.C.

They are the boys for me

They will fight; they will die;

But they never will fly.

When an enemy they see

So rise and drink this toast;

To your brothers o'er the sea;

For they are jolly good fellows,

Are the A.N.Z.A.C[39]

At half past five in the afternoon of the first official Anzac Day, 25 April 1916, Corporal Palstra and his comrades, along with Lieutenant Colonel Rankine and most of the battalion's officers, left Melbourne for Ballarat.

From Will's diary:
> Tuesday 25-4-16 Leave again for Ballarat by special train 5.30 p.m. Lt Col Rankine most of the Officers and a train load of men. A great sight, giving one remarkable feelings.

The departure was nothing short of spectacular.

The two in-line locomotives snorted steam and puffed and blew like gigantic, mettlesome draught horses eager to strain into the harness and start hauling. The entire length of the train, with all its extra carriages, was crammed with hearty young men in uniform. Their khaki-sleeved arms bristled from the windows, their shouts and whistles rang in the air.

---

39   The A.N.Z.A.C.S. Words by A.J. Graham; music by Albert H. Light. Date: circa 1914—1918.

Despite the fact that the men would be back in Melbourne in less than a week for the farewell march of the Tenth Brigade, the platform was packed with their families and friends waving hands, handkerchiefs, hats; calling out, smiling, cheering when the engine driver blew the whistle, walking alongside the train, as it began slowly to pull out from the station, breaking into a trot and then running as far as they could to the platform's end, before they had to halt and lean over the railings waving until the laden carriages dwindled from view.

Ballarat, when they arrived, was a-bustle with activity. The inhabitants were proudly organising parties to see off 'The Ballarat Battalion'.

Now that the time of embarkation was rapidly approaching, it appears that the young man suddenly found that he could not bear that final leave should really be final. He applied for leave the following weekend, and the weekend after that. He wrote to his parents every day. They were constantly sending him letters and parcels; the most recent package had contained a pair of double-knitted socks Mother had made. By now Will had begun preserving all the cherished letters from home—he decided to keep them all, every single one.

By whatever means, thankfully Will did preserve those letters, so that decades later we who came after could read them and share his experiences.

On Sunday, Will's Ballarat friends the Joyces gave a small party for him. He must have felt privileged to be the guest of honour. Except at family birthday celebrations, such distinction had probably not been bestowed on him before.

Embarkation day was drawing ever closer. It was only four weeks away.

One thing was uppermost in each man's minds whenever he thought about going to the front line. When the time came for them to be tried, would he be found wanting?

On the morning of Monday, 1 May the battalion journeyed to Melbourne to parade with the rest of the Tenth Brigade. The 37th Battalion from Seymour and the 38th from Bendigo were marching with the 39th. The 40th, trained in Tasmania, had not yet left their island home for the mainland and therefore could not participate; but in all, there were more than two thousand men on parade.

Starting from Flinders Street Railway Station the column, four abreast, proceeded through the city and received a rousing reception from the thousands who had turned out to do them honour.[40] It was the hour of glory for the Tenth Brigade; the season of their full strength and splendour. Brightly shone these stalwart young soldiers; new, untried and keen-edged as swords. Golden-throated brass sang, drums thundered like a blood-pulse, a myriad of booted feet struck the pavement with the rhythm of a giant heart beating.

A.T. Paterson, the 39th's historian, wrote, 'Only those who have taken part in an embarkation march with their own unit through their own capital city in war-time can fully realise the thrill and emotion which it all causes—the cheers and faces of the crowd, the bands playing, the fixed bayonets, the tramp of feet in step, the feeling that one has the privilege of serving with real men.'

Three battalions; rank upon rank of men, all in full uniform, complete with web equipment, with fixed bayonets standing up like a slanting forest of steel, came marching like an avalanche down the broad thoroughfare of Collins Street—where, a lifetime ago it seemed, a modest accountant had stepped out the door of the Pianola Company, his fingers ink-stained. After the months of training, of waiting, of speculation, the spectacle must have seemed slightly unreal but immensely thrilling.

Imagine:

Will takes pride in striding along in time to the band's rendition of 'Battle Hymn of the Commonwealth', keeping an eye out for the face of his mother to appear in the midst of the throng. School holidays are over, so Hettie, being a teacher, and Blanche and John, being students, are unable to be present. Will's father is away on business, but sure enough, there is Mother, moving nimbly through the crowds. She waves to him. Will manages to position himself at the outer edge of the moving column so that his mother can walk alongside him.

---

40   The 39th: The History of the 39th Battalion AIF A.T. Paterson. G.W. Green & Sons, Melbourne, 1934.

Thus, the two are able to enjoy many pleasant conversations as the troops wend their way along the route.

AWM H16126 c 1916 AIF troops marching along Elizabeth Street Melbourne before embarking on a troop transport taking them to overseas duty. (Donor A.W. Bazley)

'I am glad I found you,' says Mother, smiling up at her son. 'I just looked for your regimental flag and there you were, behind it. Now tell me, what little luxuries would you most like to take with you overseas?'

'Well, I have a sweet tooth, as you know, so some dried fruits would be nice,' Will replies. 'Oh, by the way Mum, would you mind selling my suit for me?'

Will is referring to the civilian clothes he had worn while working as an office clerk. 'I'll not be needing it in the near future, so it seems a waste to have it hanging in the wardrobe while I'm gone. The money can go into my savings account, and I can purchase a new suit when I get back.' He always makes sure he displayed an optimistic attitude when speaking to his parents.

When I get back…

'The other day Frank mentioned he would like to buy it,' Mother replies.

As a bank clerk, Frank would benefit from having a spare suit. 'Good idea!' Will says. 'He can have it at bargain rates!'

'After the march the Battalion returned to Ballarat to undergo the 'finishing touches' of training in Australia,' as Paterson recorded.

> The Salvation Army,
> The Chief Secretary's Office,
> National Headquarters,
> 69 Bourke Street, Melbourne
>
> Northcote May 3, 1916
>
> My dear Will,
>
> I have just finished the little mattress, and I believe it is a success, I wished you were here just for a moment, we should put all the cushions in and try it, now I shall wait till Saturday all being well. You can understand how I look out for these hours together, I am sure dear father will enjoy it so much, he feels as though he was quite out of it. I have firmly made up my mind to come to Ballarat on Saturday but if we shall stay over for Sunday seems to depend upon circumstances, however we are making plans to see you again.
>
> We were very lucky on Monday to see so much of one another, so there is nearly always something to be thankful for, even when things not all together move after our own wishes.

Your first letter arrived here Monday afternoon. It was very cheerful to read, I wonder how the little party went off. In one way I am very sorry your camp was so far from Melbourne, we might have seen one another a lot more, but on the other hand, I am so pleased you found such nice friends, and that in connection with the corps you made quite a name for yourself, somebody told father already about your singing, and he was so proud to hear about you, and how you took your stand. I am sure it has done a lot of good.

Your second letter came this afternoon, no wire came till up to now, I shall be looking out tomorrow. I am glad you feel so hopeful about the future, dear father felt lifted up ever so much after reading your letter, may the Lord grant that all will be well and that a useful and happy life may be before you, and that the world may be better and wiser through all the courage and self-sacrifice shown by thousands and thousands.

Now let me think what I wanted to tell you.

1. I have been to Alpha for the photos. The soonest I could get them is today after eight. I did not pay them, it might slacken his efforts, but told him I should be there to fetch them. I also told him about the stripes.

2. Frank has paid me £3 for your suit, we put it on your bankbook, so that young man is out of debt. He has got a chance to become fourth teller next week. It takes most of them three years. Has father already told you about what he heard about Charlie's exam. in Duntroon? Not to mention names —someone told him, that they were classed in 5 degrees, and that Charles belonged to the very few in the fourth, he had done exceptionally well. You can just fancy how he looked when Dad told him. His commission is only a question of days. He was here this afternoon, and what seldom happens I was out to a meeting (Col. D.) so I did not see him. May be that he is coming

with us on Saturday. Johnnie went off to school on Monday, and so did the girls, so I am by myself again. There is however, so much planned for a day, that one forgets to feel lonely.

Work is a great blessing after all.

I shall get the wool for the mittens tomorrow, I hope to have them ready beginning next week. I was glad to hear the socks answered the purpose, it was my own invention. Miss Hewitt brought me a book with patterns tonight so I shall know all about it in future.

I better say goodnight now, it is already late, everybody is in bed, that's just the time when I like to have a little chat with you. I hope all plans will come right for Saturday.

God bless and keep you,

your loving,

Mother.

I got a postcard from Auntie Lous, she is in Paris in France. I'll bring him [sic] with me to read.

Leave-approval came through, and Will dispatched a wire to his parents with the good news. He was home on Saturday 6th May for the weekend. To his delight, Dad was home too. Will gazed critically at the photographic portrait, which everyone said they admired, but perhaps he could not help feeling that he looked rather young for an NCO, because soon afterwards he grew a moustache, which made him look a little older.

His parents gave him a Box Brownie camera to take with him overseas, so that he could send photos back to them.

There were sixteen days left until embarkation when, on Thursday 11 May a huge farewell concert was given in honour of the 39th. It took place at Ballarat's 'Coliseum Picture Palace', at that time the largest cinema venue in Australia. This spectacular venue, which could hold eight thousand people, had taken only seventy-seven days to build in 1908, and had opened on 29 September 1909.[41]

On the outside of the building the upper storey was obscured by gigantic billboards advertising:

PATHE's PICTURES

THE HALL OF EASE

CHANGE OF PROGRAM WEDNESDAYS AND SATURDAYS

The ground floor's exterior was covered with huge, coloured posters depicting scenes from films currently showing, with ticket prices painted in between. The motion picture this week might have been, for example, Australasian Films' feature-length production, 'The Hero of the Dardanelles',[42] the story of a young man who enlists in the AIF, is sent to Egypt, fights a Turk barehanded at Gallipoli, and after being wounded is repatriated to Australia where he marries his sweetheart, Lily, and lives happily ever after. The film ends with a call to Australian men to do their duty and join up.

Films made by The Salvation Army were once shown in the Coliseum. It is a little-known fact that at one time The Salvation Army was the largest film producer in existence. Salvationists in Australia were among the world's first and most prolific film makers. Coincidentally, the whole film-making enterprise had actually begun in Ballarat, at the close of the 19th century. In 1892 a Salvationist named Joe Perry bought a 'Magic Lantern' to

---

41   Since the building of the Coliseum, due to the growing popularity of films, two more 'Houses of Dreams' had opened in Ballarat—'The Alfred Hall' and 'Her Majesty's'. The Coliseum was destroyed by fire in 1936. In the 21st century the only legacy of the Coliseum building in Ballarat appears to be a short, narrow road named Coliseum Walk.

42   'The Hero of the Dardanelles' can be viewed on the Internet at http://australianscreen.com.au/titles/hero-of-the-dardanelles/.

present slide shows, enhanced with music and sound effects, to raise funds for the Army's Ballarat 'Prison Gate' home.

Hearing of the Magic Lantern's popularity, The Salvation Army brought Mr Perry to Melbourne. The success of his shows led to the creation of the Army's 'Limelight Department', whose job it was to make and present slideshows. The title 'Limelight' was inspired by the name of the outdated light source once used for slide projection and theatre spotlights.

The Limelight Department's slide-shows were highly popular. They were accompanied by music and sound effects, and occasionally by special effects such as flashes of 'lightning'—which was terribly exciting for the audiences. They were shown all around Australia and New Zealand. Money raised by the shows was put towards the Army's work among the needy.

When motion pictures first appeared in Australia in 1896, they astounded audiences all over the country, so Australian Salvation Army HQ immediately authorised the Limelight Department to purchase equipment for making and projecting 'actualities', as those early films were called. A film studio was built at the back of the Melbourne Headquarters building in Bourke Street, and after a year or two of hard work,[43] Limelight had created Australia's first fictional narrative films. They included such plots as the story of a starving man who was imprisoned for stealing a loaf of bread and who, on his release, was cared for by The Salvation Army's Prison Gate Brigade.

The film that really made an impression on everyone was 'Soldiers Of The Cross', which was designed as a recruiting show to attract new people to the new officer training garrison in East Melbourne. Will had only been eight years old and living overseas with his family when it premiered at the Melbourne Town Hall,[44] but no doubt his parents read about it in the *War Cry*. It was more than a film—there were sound effects and hundreds of hand-coloured glass slides, and scores of actors playing the roles of Christian martyrs. The scenes

---

43   May 1898

44   'Soldiers of the Cross' premiered on September 13, 1900

of martyrdom were pretty gruesome. There were people being thrown into lime pits, jabbed by Roman spears, tied to stakes to be burnt, eaten by lions or drowned. The audience was deeply affected. Some even wept.

In 1906 Herbert Booth became leader of The Salvation Army in Australasia. He swiftly grasped the possibilities of moving pictures as a powerful evangelical force and a way to raise funds. Branches of the Limelight Department were established across Australia and in New Zealand. By mid-1907, films were shown weekly in Army centres in the largest cities, and touring companies continued to give shows throughout the country. Altogether, The Salvation Army made about three hundred films between 1898 and 1909.[45] After twenty years of steady growth, the Army's film operations reached the height of their success in 1910.

So what happened? Why did it all stop?

Because in that year a new leader of The Salvation Army in Australasia was appointed. Commissioner James Hay shut down the Limelight Department because he claimed the looseness of morals in the film industry was reflecting badly on Salvation Army presentations. He said that the cinema, as conducted by The Salvation Army, had led to weakness, and a lightness incompatible with true Salvationism. Therefore, he said, it must be completely ended. His pronouncement on the Limelight Department was, 'Nowhere do I see it recorded in the Gospels that the graces bestowed by the Spirit include the power to amuse'.'

Commissioner Hay had made his decree, and all Salvationists must heed it, regardless of their own opinion on the matter. But the closing of the Limelight Department involved considerable costs, and it took years for many Salvation Army centres to return to normal after losing such an important source of income.

By 1916 Salvationist Headquarters' official line was that cinema was forbidden.

---

45 Information about The Salvation Army's Limelight Department comes from http://www.abc.net.au/limelight/default.htm

Will had not set foot in a Picture House for several years, and neither had anyone in his family or circle of acquaintance. The once thriving film studio at the back of his father's office in Bourke Street had been closed down two years before the Palstras had even arrived in the country.

On Thursday 11 May at the Coliseum in Ballarat, in through the main doors poured the men of the 39th, proceeding along the plush red carpet that led down the centre of the lobby into the vast auditorium. Potted palms and marble busts on tall plinths lined the entrance hall. The walls, covered with elaborately figured wallpaper, were decorated with pictures of idyllic landscapes in carved and gilded frames and, at intervals, ornate corbels supporting parian figurines in flowing draperies. Heavy velvet curtains festooned side portals, and a tall oval mirror in a gorgeously embellished frame reflected the masses of men in uniform who came thronging forward. Inside, vast numbers of seats in curved rows faced a wide stage, with an organ to one side and an orchestra pit below. Upstairs galleries lined the side walls.

Visualise an army officer appearing on the stage, accompanied by an eruption of whistling and cheering. He commands everyone to stand up for the singing of the National Anthem. The orchestra plays an introduction, and presently the roof of the house almost lifts off with the power of the voices of seven hundred men as they roared out the well-known words—'God save our gracious King...'

That evening there were no films shown in the Picture House. Instead, the troops were presented with a most excellent and diverting concert, incorporating an abundance of music, singing and dancing, humorous acts, colourful costumes, spectacular lighting, stirring speeches and everything required to amuse and entertain. Neither trouble nor expense had been spared in making the function a success.[46]

---

46   The 39th: The History of the 39th Battalion AIF A.T. Paterson. G.W. Green & Sons, Melbourne, 1934.

A few days later *The Argus*[47] would report—

> CITIZENS' "SEND-OFF."
>
> BALLARAT Thursday —
>
> Ballarat will long remember the godspeed which it expressed to the 39th Battalion in the Coliseum tonight. The building was crowded and the utmost enthusiasm characterised the gathering, over which Mr F R Coldham, chairman of the Citizens' Committee, presided. The soldiers were heartily greeted as they filed into the galleries which had been reserved for them.
>
> The acting State Commandant Brigadier General Williams said that the 39th would always be regarded by Ballarat people as their own regiment, even although all the men in it were not drawn from the district.
>
> The Premier (Sir Alexander Peacock) said that Australian boys had done well and would continue to do so (Applause). The pledge of the Empire to redress wrongs was the obligation of every part of it. The enemy was not to be beaten by calling him Hun and Vandal: the sacrifice had to be made and the men of the 39th were making the sacrifice (Cheers). It was something to be proud of to know that our people were responding to the call and the best news that we could send across the sea was that Australia was continuing to find men and money to carry out her fair share of the war (Applause). To the men of the battalion he would say — "You go with our best wishes. God bless you."

The camp was alive with the news of the arrival of Australian and New Zealand troops on the Western Front. One newspaper reported:

---

47   The Argus (Melbourne, Vic. : 1848-1954) Friday 12 May 1916, page 8

```
POPULARITY IN FRANCE

A correspondent at the British head-quarters writes that
never since the first British expeditionary force secretly
entered France had there been a less obtrusive entry than
that of the Anzacs. They have already accomplished a record
of quick popularity with the country folk, among whom they
are billeted.

Apart from the claims of admiration owing to their physique
and coquettish hats, which have a particular charm for the
village maidens, the Anzacs appeal to the inhabitants'
hearts because they have travelled thousands of miles to
fight for them.

The Anzacs now know the Germans are tougher customers than
Ibrahim and Abdul, while on his side, the Boche has doubtless
conceived a much-enhanced respect for the wallabies. All the
German attempts to shake the Anzacs' spirits by alternately
cajoling and strafing have ended distinctly in favour of the
Anzacs.

Already the Maori warriors are a parable among the children
for good humour and liberality. The chocolate shops are
a real study in telegraphy. It is amusing to observe how
thoroughly the soldiers and youngsters understand one
another, despite the linguistic shortcomings. The Anzacs
are unanimous that they are having a good time.

'We are amongst the people," said a New Zealander,
contrasting his present existence with the pent-up acres of
baked Turkish soil.[48]
```

Across southern Australia the last leaves of autumn were falling. In a few days' time, winter would officially begin. The days were shorter, the nights were cooler. And soon the 39th would be setting out on that long journey across the winter sea.

---

48 Examiner (Launceston, Tas. : 1900 - 1954). Monday 15 May 1916 page 5

1916: Dash and Determination | 3: Embarkation

Northcote,

23 May, 1916

My dear Boy,

I have been sitting alone in the dining room for a little while, the rest of the family having gone to bed. Of course it needed a little persuasion to get dear Dad upstairs, but it did not help me to get on, him looking at my hands with such a tired look on his face, he had been more than busy today. I wanted just my own time to finish the little things I promised you. What do you think of the little case for the locket, I have lined it with cotton wool and a bit of silk, I should say it is practically waterproof. I hope it fits.

Your name on the piece of cloth is not up to much, perhaps because I did it [embroidered it] last, never mind I'll make you a couple and send them up.

Put it once more on a piece of paper how you want it to be done. [Will must have asked for name tags which he could sew onto his garments to identify them.]

Now while my hands were busy my thoughts were all the time with you. I could not help thinking, that although my head is sad now the moment of parting has come, that I had so many reasons to be thankful for. You have been always such a good son to us, and we have so many reasons to be proud of you. Not one moment came ever any doubt in my heart about anything concerning your character. I know you do love God and I could not think that you would ever do anything that was low or mean. What a blessing and comfort brings this to my soul.

I do love you as ever a mother has loved her first born, and my prayers will go up to our heavenly Father, that he may shield you and keep you from dangers known and unknown and that he may bring you out of all this unharmed in body and soul.

Perhaps I shall have a chance of giving you once more a farewell kiss, maybe only a glance at a distance. In fact we have said goodbye or rather, so the Lord will, au revoir for a short time. May God's blessing rest upon you my dear Will, be sure you have got mine.

Your ever loving,

Mother.

The Ballarat Courier, Wednesday 24 May 1916 Page 4

```
THANKS FROM THE 39TH

To the Editor of 'The Courier." Sir, — Allow me to heartily
thank the good people of Ballarat for the magnificent
treatment meted out to the boys of the 39th Battalion during
their sojourn in the Ballarat Camp. The boys are under a
deep debt of obligation to all those ladies and gentlemen
who so generously donated their time, money, and services
in promoting the welfare of the boys, and if they could hear
the kindly sentiments that have been expressed from time
to time they would feel compensated for the sacrifices that
have been made. On the eve of our departure from amongst
you I take this opportunity on behalf of the boys to once
again thank the citizens of Ballarat.

— Yours. &c. ONE OF THE BOYS, 39TH (BALLARAT) BATTALION.
```

Will was back in camp, where everyone was keyed up. The atmosphere was feverish. 'We're off at last!' was the cry. The men were eager to go, ready to apply themselves to the work for which they had been preparing themselves for months, yet at the same time they were looking around at the wide, eucalyptus tree covered landscape under blue skies as if they saw Australia for the first time. Suddenly it all seemed so precious.

They were all given new regimental numbers—Corporal Palstra's was 555—and on Tuesday sea-kit bags were issued.

The following notice was handed out:

> This paper is to be considered by each soldier as confidential, and to be kept in his Active Service Pay Book.

> You are ordered abroad as a soldier of the King to help our French comrades against the invasion of a common Enemy. You have to perform a task which will need your courage, your energy, your patience. Remember that the honour of the British Army depends on your individual conduct. It will be your duty not only to set an example of discipline and perfect steadiness under fire but

also to maintain the most friendly relations with those whom you are helping in this struggle. The operations in which you are engaged will, for the most part, take place in a friendly country, and you can do your own country no better service than in showing yourself in France and Belgium in the true character of a British soldier.

Be invariably courteous, considerate and kind. Never do anything likely to injure or destroy property, and always look upon looting as a disgraceful act. You are sure to meet with a welcome and to be trusted; your conduct must justify that welcome and that trust. Your duty cannot be done unless your health is sound. So keep constantly on your guard against any excesses. In this new experience you may find temptations both in wine and women. You must entirely resist both temptations, and, while treating all women with perfect courtesy, you should avoid any intimacy.

Do your duty bravely,

Fear God,

Honour the King.

KITCHENER,

Field-Marshal.

Having folded these papers into their pay-books—probably not without cracking a joke or two about having to leave some of their more licentious mates behind—the men produced their 'pocket housewives' and got busy stitching their new regimental numbers on to their bags, web equipment and other paraphernalia for identification purposes.

A small package from Mother arrived for Will, with a letter enclosed. Inside the parcel was a beautifully made case, just the right size to hold the miniature-containing locket that Will's parents had given him. His name was embroidered on it.

With the greatest care Will placed the locket in its new receptacle, tucked it away safely and commenced to write a note of thanks to his mother.

Wednesday 24 May was Empire Day, the birthday of Queen Victoria, an annual holiday which had been proclaimed after her death in 1901. The celebration gave Britain's subjects around the globe an opportunity to display their pride in belonging to the Empire. Throughout the British Dominions the day was marked with street parades, dressing in costume, inspirational speeches by statesmen, fireworks displays in back gardens and gathering at community bonfires. Empire Day was celebrated no less in Ballarat than in any other township. Will took some more photographs and finally used up the whole roll of film. At camp there were speeches and solemn flag-raisings.

Far away at the Royal Military College, Duntroon, on 25 May Will's brother Charles filled out a form applying for a commission in the AIF. That same day the 39th Battalion's baggage guard, 'lustily cheered by all who remained in camp, left for Port Melbourne'.[49]

Next day was the last the troops would spend in camp. Ballarat gave them a concert party to chase away the sadness of that final night.

The clock ticked over midnight. Hardly anyone had caught a wink of sleep.

A young regimental signaller called Clive Blackburn was among the men of the 39th. In civilian life he had worked at the railway offices at Melbourne's Flinders Street Station. He penned long and informative letters to his mother, in the notebook he always carried with him.[50] He begins with an evocative description of morning at the Ballarat training camp on the day of departure.

---

49   Paterson

50   He titled his record, 'The Voyage of the 39th Battalion 10th Infantry Paraphrased and quoted from TBde on the HMAT 'Ascanius' A11 to 'Somewhere' on Active Service', by L/cpl Clive Blackburn, Regimental Signal Sect. no. 257, 27th May 1916.

'27.5.16

'Reveille at 1am and breakfast at 2 am. The fall in was carried out in silence and in darkness. Every man realised the purpose for which he was falling in, and in spite of the excitement which possessed every man, all was carried out coolly.

'The battalion marched out of the Showgrounds for the last time at 3.45am.

'The residents all came out to the doors and gates in all manner of attire to wave farewell. As many of the men remarked, 'no one would be late for work at Ballarat that day'.

'Even the patients in the hospital were awake. [As many as could get on their feet were up and about.] Sturt St was fairly crowded. Hand-shakes were given by many young ladies, and when we got to the station, kisses were given freely. Fortunately I refrained from such luxuries.'

Paterson wrote that the Battalion, headed by its band, marched through the streets of Ballarat well before sunrise, '...while thousands of people lined the route. The onlookers and the men of the battalion, true to their national tradition, tried to stifle their emotion, but sadness tinged the air. Scenes of touching incidents along the route made this short march an unforgettable experience for all.

A reporter from the Ballarat Star wrote,

```
"Departure of 39th Battalion.⁵¹

"In the "wee sma' hours" of Saturday morning the 39th
Ballarat Battalion took its departure for Melbourne. There
was great activity at the camp shortly after midnight,
and excitement reigned high when reveille sounded. The
```

---

51   The Ballarat Star, 29th May 1916

> Battalion Band was playing patriotic music, and the clear, frosty air carried the musical strains near and far.
>
> "After a hot breakfast had been served out to the men, they were formed into line and marched away from the scene of many hard, but happy, days of training. Headed by the band, they proceeded via Drummond Street north, Sturt Street and Lydiard Street, to the Western station, where there were hundreds of people to see them off.
>
> "Two special trains had been provided for the troops, who, though glad to be taking their departure for the more serious part of warfare, were manifestly affected at having to leave near and dear ones. The departure of the first train, which was timed for 4.40, was delayed about half an hour.52 In the meantime the band played lively airs, including "Australia Will be There," "Keep Your Eyes on Germany," "The Marsellaise," "The Girl I Left Behind Me."
>
> "As the train steamed out of the station boisterous cheers were given for the men by the large crowd in the vicinity of the platform. At about a quarter to six o'clock the second special took its departure. There was an even larger attendance of people, who were equally enthusiastic in their send-off to the soldiers. xix

Will's Ballarat friends and acquaintances were among the crowds at the station who waved and cheered as the troop train slowly steamed away from the platform. The men leaning from the open windows turned their heads to look back until the station was out of sight.

Clive Blackburn wrote: 'The train journey down [to Melbourne] was very quiet. Most men [had] had no rest and nearly all 'tried to sleep'.'

---

52   The newspapers report the departure time as 5:10 am, whereas the official record 'The 39th' states it as 'punctually at 4 am'. It is easier to believe the journalist, who had no reason to misrepresent the facts.

Some of the men had smuggled the bulldog that was the battalion's mascot on board the train, vowing they would take him with them, for they couldn't bear to be parted from the good-natured fellow. Even the dog was quiet on the trip.

What a scene unfolded at Port Melbourne that afternoon! Around midday, the troop trains drew up alongside His Majesty's Australian Troopship 'A11', the official designation of the steamship *Ascanius*. The troopship *Barambah*, 'A37'—formerly the German ship *Hobart*—was berthed behind the *Ascanius*. The men of the 39th paraded on the pier and rolls were called. This would be their last roll call in Australia.

A photographer, his camera mounted on a tall tripod, was busy taking official snaps of officers on their own, officers in groups, bands, platoons and entire companies.

PB0140 AWM Australia: Victoria, Melbourne, Port Melbourne 27 May 1916 HMAT Ascanius (A11).

PB0141 AWM Australia: Victoria, Melbourne, Port Melbourne 27 May 1916 HMAT Ascanius (A11).

Temporary wooden barriers separated the onlookers from the troops—or were intended to. The text of 'The 39th: The History of the 39th Battalion A.I.F' implies that there was no contact between the public and the troops before the men boarded the ship, however Will writes in a letter that he handed his parents a roll of undeveloped film at Port Melbourne.

Somehow, experts as they were at navigating crowds, the Palstras found their son on the crowded pier, and he found them. For the briefest of stolen moments they spoke to each other over the barriers and touched hands. He passed them an envelope containing the roll of film, and Mother handed him a small package.

'Good luck, dear boy,' Mother says. 'Send us a cable as soon as you can!'

They can hardly bear to let go of him.

PB1297 AWM Troop transport ship—Infantry waiting to embark. Exact date unknown.

PB0129 AWM Australia: Victoria, Melbourne, Port Melbourne

27 May 1916 HMAT Ascanius (A11).

PB0132 AWM Australia: Victoria, Melbourne, Port Melbourne 27 May 1916

PB0161 AWM Australia: Victoria, Melbourne, Port Melbourne 27 May 1916 Troops on board HMAT Ascanius (A11).

PB0135 AWM 27 May 1916 Australia: Victoria, Melbourne, Port Melbourne HMAT Ascanius (A11).

PB0146 AWM 27 May 1916 Australia: Victoria, Melbourne, Port Melbourne HMAT Ascanius (A11).

Lance-corporal Clive Blackburn of the 39th's Regimental Signal Section embarked on the same voyage as Will, although it is doubtful whether the two ever met. The words Blackburn wrote in his notebook provide much valuable information about the boarding of the *Ascanius* and the subsequent voyage.

The 39th Battalion, more than a thousand men, waited on Station Pier. At last, after fully two hours had elapsed, orders were shouted above the din. Watched by senior officers standing on either side, hundreds of baggage-laden men marched up the gangplanks. It was a long time before all were aboard.

Will, standing on the crowded deck of the steamship, shoulder to shoulder with his comrades, gazing down at Station Pier where his loved ones were gathered.

After the ship's crew had retracted the gangways the gates opened and the families and other well-wishers came flooding to get as close as possible to the ship.

'Back through the big gates,' wrote Clive Blackburn, 'we see the silent, sober crowd waiting. Suddenly the gates swing open and the crowd charges onto the wharf. We coo-ee and call and they answer. Streamers are thrown from the wharf and we catch them. We're a happy-go-lucky, carefree lot.'

The mood was a mixture of tremendous excitement, high spirits and sadness. The 39th Battalion's Official History tells us that, 'From every vantage point on shore and aboard, friends, relations and sweethearts bade each other farewell. The band played. Messages were written and exchanged under great difficulties. Paper streamers formed a last tangible link between those on shore and aboard.'

The air was filled with shouts and flourished handkerchiefs, and even tiny impromptu gifts lofted through the air.

Blackburn gives us insight into the way the men masked the grief of parting with ostentatious flippancy and euphoric displays. 'Cracking hardy' was the term they used for the joking and banter in which they engaged when they were at their most miserable. He writes:

Down on the wharf we see the girls who've caught our spirit. We see two older women with eyes ever searching, searching for a last glimpse of a loved face. They're the mothers and wives, the silent sufferers amongst the seemingly carefree throng. Men are there too, brothers and pals calling and cheering to us and dads proudly erect and calm. Every now and again, a flutter of movement that we try not to see: a mother, wife, sister or sweetheart who couldn't stand the pretence any longer and is being taken away to the rear. A few minutes and she's gamely fought down her sorrow and is working her way steadily forward again, smiling. Brave-hearted women of Australia, playing their part as they've played it from the beginning. You'll do us.'[53]"

Unlike Corporal Palstra, signaller Clive Blackburn had not been lucky enough to get an opportunity to speak with his own family members, who were assembled among the crowd on the wharf. He had to content himself with throwing small mementos to them from the deck. The other men on board were tossing little impromptu gifts to their loved ones—rummaging in their pockets for coins, pencils—anything they could possibly fling down to the people on the wharf; for this final exchange of physical items was the last link between them, maybe forever.

Lance-corporal Blackburn was infected by the mood. Feverishly, he searched his pockets. On locating a pencil and a halfpenny, he drew back his arm and hurled them with as much force and accuracy as possible. His heart was in his mouth—what if they should fall down the crack between the ship and the pier? Somehow the loss of those last-minute keepsakes would be crushing. His face must have been wreathed in smiles when a family member deftly caught the souvenirs in mid-air. In return, Blackburn's family threw small keepsakes and other gifts back to him.

---

53 'You'll do' — a term of high praise.

He later wrote:

> I was bitterly disappointed at not being able to speak to you all and I know how you all felt. It took me all my time to keep from howling. Never mind, I was glad one streamer lasted and that you got that ½ penny and pencil. How they did not go down a crack I don't know, also I don't know how I caught the cake of Spearmint Gran threw. I've put that aside for an emergency ration. Gran's 'hanky' I kept always.

The departure of a fully laden troopship on a Saturday afternoon was a fine spectacle. The big steamer with masts fore and aft, once a merchant vessel of the Blue Funnel Line, towered over the scene. Every section of her superstructure was crammed with soldiers on the starboard side overlooking the crowded pier. *En masse* they leaned from the windows and from among the life boats and pushed against the railings, occupying every available position along the five-hundred-foot length of the vessel, so that some might have thought it a wonder *SS Ascanius*[54] with so much weight all on one side, did not capsize. Some men had even climbed up the rigging. The band played, the crowds cheered. From ship to shore, messages were being written and exchanged under great difficulties.

Down below decks in the engine room—a hot, cramped world of pipes, valves, gauges, pumps and motors—the crew was raising steam, ready for the start. Under the watchful eye of the First Assistant Engineer, firemen smeared with coal-dust were stoking rows of blazing furnaces. Oilers were busy lubricating and checking the bearings of the gigantic main engine. The increasing heat in the boilers was bringing the steam up to pressure. As the engines idled, the ship throbbed with a low, almost subsonic rhythm, like the beating of a heart.

No matter why they were leaving, no matter who they were, this was the separation of people from their loved ones; in particular of mothers from their children, perhaps the hardest parting of all.

---

54   SS: Steamship. This is the way Will recorded the ship's title in his pocket diary at the time. It has more recently been recorded as HMAT: His Majesty's Australian Troopship, and in his later 'Diary of War Experiences' Will calls it H.M.T.S. 'A11'.

All at once the ship's crew began to move about in an energetic and busy manner. They released the end of the cables on board, letting them run out and slither overboard. At 1.20 p.m. the grating sounds of enormous winches starting to rotate proclaimed that the time for farewells had ended.

Suddenly, louder than all, piercing through and beyond, came the deep booming call of the ship herself, crying out to leave; the sound that heralded departure.

Three times the ship uttered her powerful steam-driven call, and other steamers in the vicinity sounded their sirens in answer to her mournful cry. Seamen removed the gangways, while longshoremen freed the great mooring hawsers, as thick as a man's arm. Then *Ascanius's* ropes were cast off, and as the sturdy little tugs began to haul on her chains slowly, ever so slowly, she commenced to move sideways.

The men aboard sang, cheered and waved. 'Good bye! Good bye!'

The gap between ship and wharf widened, and as it did so the men holding streamers let them unroll to their fullest extent so that they might not tear; but now a broad strip of water showed, and now the fragile paper strips were breaking, one by one, swathes of pale green and pink and yellow dropping lazily through the air, the ripped ends falling into the sea like strips torn from a pastel rainbow—the heartstrings of bereft communities.

While the gap grew wider and wider a long cheer swelled from the crowd, and a subtle swell rose beneath the iron hull as the outer muscles of the ocean began to flex and the tugs turned the vessel's bows southwards.

Slowly, *Ascanius* drew away from the land.

Clive Blackburn: 'We're on the first stage of our great adventure. Cheers, coo-ees and the cock-a-doodle-do of harbour craft intermingle in a grand finale. Men, perched high in the rigging, commence to sing and soon the whole ship unites in a last song of farewell...'

Men crowded the weather-deck, their eyes hungrily fixed on the wharf where the colourful crowd jostled and waved. For most, it was the saddest sight they had ever seen.

The khaki clad figures aboard became more indistinct to those ashore; the faces of those left behind dwindled out of recognition.

Now it was time for *HMAT Ascanius* to strike out under her own steam. Down in her belly, bells jangled as the engine room telegraph rang for half speed ahead. The idling turbines laboured into action. Firemen worked hard, sweat running off their bodies in rivulets. One opened a firebox door, a second expertly tossed in a shovelful of coal, and the first smartly shut and latched the door to keep in the heat. Fireboxes glowed with flame, pressure soared, pumps pounded, water seethed in the boilers. Massive pistons oscillated inside vertically oriented cylinders, slide valves opened and closed, turbines spun, the crankshaft turned and the gigantic propeller began to rotate.

With her funnels pumping out thick smoke the *Ascanius* ploughed across Port Phillip Bay, heading for the bay's entrance, Port Phillip Heads, beyond which lay the open sea. A long fringe of broken paper streamers trailed into the wavelets on her starboard side.

She glided smoothly, outlined against low banks of cloud underlit with the warm glow of the setting sun. A dense plume stretched horizontally behind her, parallel to the sea, as if clouds had snagged themselves on her funnels.

Lance-corporal Blackburn:

> 1.30pm. As the boat steamed away, it was a fine sight. Our boat must have looked well, but the blaze of colour on the pier looked fine. Naturally the sight was the saddest one could witness, but soldiers are most unhappy when they're 'cracking hardy'. There was a good bit of 'cracking hardy' while that boat moved off. Some sang, some smiled, some sang out, some remained silent. If I'd have opened my mouth I would have cried.
>
> It was not until I went below and opened your [his mother's] parcels that I realised it was your last gift. Then the tears did come up. Most [of the other men] were the same. The reaction set in then. It was only for a while and [then] all settled down.'

At 5.30 pm, just after sunset, the steamship passed through Port Phillip Heads. Both forts on each side signalled farewell, after which Fort Nepean fort flashed their searchlights, the tall beams standing up stark and bright into the evening skies, and Queenscliff followed their example. It was a spectacular salute.

At 6p.m. the pilot left the steamship, taking with him a few letters for home and the stowaway some of the men had managed to smuggle aboard—the much-loved bull-dog mascot of the 39th Battalion. (Other battalions were able to get away with smuggling their animal mascots on board their transports. At least one kangaroo left its native shores, never to return.)

In the gathering dusk, *Ascanius* received a signal-lamp message flashed from the pilot ship—'Good-bye and Good Luck.' HMAT A.11 then headed towards the Cape Otway lighthouse.

Ascanius, a vessel of some 11,000 tons, was carrying one thousand, seven hundred and sixty-four people. Crowded on board with the men of the 39th and the staff of their headquarters—headed by Lieutenant Colonel Rankine, DSO—were the staff of the Tenth Infantry Brigade Headquarters, the First Reinforcements Tenth Machine Gun Company, the Third Divisional Signal Company, a detail of the Tenth Field Ambulance, and the First Reinforcements, 39th and 37th Battalions.

They were all on their way to the 'Great Adventure.'

'In 1916 and 1917 more than two thousand ordinary men, including reinforcements, left their families and communities in Victoria as members of the 39th Battalion of the Australian Imperial Forces. Four hundred did not return. Of those that did return, wounded and scarred forever, few told of what they had seen.'[55]

We've left our dear old homeland,
Our parents, sweethearts, all,
We could not stay while every day,
Would see our comrades fall
The glorious ambition,
Which spares not friend or foe
Has dared our might, so now to fight
Australians all, we go

Chorus:
So farewell my sunny land
And farewell love to you
On land or sea, it seems to me

---

55 Source: The 39th. http://the39th.googlepages.com

I see your eyes of blue.
But though my country claims my heart
And lives maybe of some
There's a happy day not far away
In the days that are to come

There's times when hearts are burdened
And fortune seems unkind
And memories bring a cruel sting
To every anxious mind
'Tis you who fight the battle
Who watch and wait and pray
And so for you we'll dare and do

56   'In The Days That Are to Come', By Sidney B Young (4/4/1916) Sidney Bond Young was a bricklayer by trade. Born near Queenbeyan, NSW, he was 21 years of age when he enlisted on 9th August 1915 in the 12th Reinforcements, 4th Battalion AIF. He later transferred to the 36th Battalion and was a bandsman in the Battalion Band.

Part VI
1916: Voyage Across the World

1916: Voyage Across the World | 1: The Voyage Begins

We are not out for conquest, for we have heaps of room

Where stately gums are growing and the golden wattles bloom

We're leaving dear Australia because the cannon's roar

Of overbearing foemen call us to England's shore.

We Australian lads will very gladly share

Any dangers loved old England has to bear

Long before the rattle of her drums sound anywhere

We're on the move for the country we love

We Australians will be there.[57]

Two authorities were responsible for the transport of the AIF to Europe—the Australian Naval Board and the British Admiralty. The Naval Board set about obtaining merchant

---

57 Australia Will be There: Australia's War Song. 1914 - 1916? Written by John Beukers, composed by Harold Betteridge.

ships to make up the convoy while the Admiralty marshalled the warships to escort them. Merchant ships were requisitioned, but work was necessary to make them suitable for the task. As C.W. Bean's Official History explains:

> 'The process of conversion entailed alterations of a very drastic character. In nearly every vessel the whole of the passenger accommodation had to be gutted, and often the electric wiring and water supply systems had to be dislocated and renewed; further the galley and lavatory accommodation needed much enlargement.'[58]

To deal with the problem of transporting thousands of Australian men and horses, not to mention tons of equipment across the world to take part in the Great War, the Australian Naval Board requisitioned numerous merchant ships.

> Conversion plans were prepared as soon as a ship had been assessed as suitable, so that once her current cargo had been discharged fitting out of the vessel could begin immediately. Modification work entailed the gutting of all passenger accommodation, and included the addition of galleys, latrines, hospitals, troop deck fittings and horse stalls.
>
> The troopships might be ready for embarkation but with the whereabouts of several German warships uncertain, Imperial authorities remained unwilling to risk their passage across the Indian Ocean until a sufficiently powerful naval escort could be assembled. The Transport Branch of the Navy Department eventually arranged for the requisition of 74 troop transports and, over the course of the war, 44 convoys ferried some 337,000 men and 27,000 horses from Australia to the European theatre.
>
> None of those [passengers or crew] carried was ever lost to enemy action while on passage.'[59]

---

58   CW Bean Vol IX, 1993, p.408

59   'Australian Sea Transport 1914', Semaphore, Issue 05, April 2008, Royal Australian Navy

In addition to troop decks, the refitted ships also contained baggage racks, bedding and blanket stores, dispensaries, ammunition magazines, pantries, detention cells and canteens. In all ships, additional deck houses had to be erected to provide space for washing basins, showers and latrines.

The provision of adequate galley accommodation was a matter which at first caused the authorities some anxiety. None of the ships had previously been called on to cater for such large numbers of person, and consequently new ranges, steam boilers and steam cookers of the standard passenger ship pattern had to be provided. Owing to the urgent need of cargo space to take foodstuffs from Australia, the insulated spaces and refrigerated holds on board were left intact.

During the Great War, the technology of refrigeration allowed frozen meat to be carried by sea from Australia to England or the Middle East, but not all troopships had this kind of machinery on board. 'If the vessel in which the troops were carried was not supplied with refrigerating appliances, so that livestock for meat supplies had to be taken and fed… an additional sum was paid [to the ship's owners] to cover cost of forage and wages etc. of slaughtermen and butchers.'[60]

Dismantled steam cranes lay deep in the cargo holds, ready to be put together when they were needed for loading and unloading in port. The ballast tanks of the vessels were utilised for the storage of fresh water, and complete services of both fresh and salt water were provided by means of special piping and connections, fresh water being laid on to all troop decks.[61]

Officers were given first class, and senior NCOs second class cabins. At on-board shops known as 'canteens', the men could buy biscuits, tobacco and tinned goods. The sale or

---

60   Sea Transport of the AIF. Greville Tregarthen.

61   Source: Sea Transport of the AIF. Greville Tregarthen, Naval Transport Branch, (no date). Held at Australian War Memorial Archives.

supply of intoxicants on board was strictly prohibited, excepting only when ordered by the Senior Medical Officer for medical purposes.[62]

On 'troopers' like the *Ascanius*, men lived on the troop decks. These were constructed in what was formerly hold space, and were chiefly remarkable for the kind of mess tables which were installed. The tables, which accommodated twenty men each, were placed on either side, along the entire length of the deck, leaving a broad aisle between, in which the arm racks—stands for holding weapons such as rifles—were positioned. Long benches provided seating, while directly overhead, hammocks and equipment racks were slung from hooks. At either end of the decks stood bins in which the hammocks were stowed when not in use. The decks were lit by electricity and ventilated by hatchways, and by canvas ventilators arranged on the same principle as the ordinary ship's ventilators.[63]

It was not only allied vessels that were pressed into service at the outset of the Great War. At the commencement of hostilities in 1914, Australian waters harboured twenty-eight vessels owned by the enemy. These were promptly interned, and their German and Austrian crews removed. Before the crews were taken off the ships, however, they tried to wreck the machinery, resorting to many strange and cunning devices. The allies had to make sure there were no hidden traps on board the commandeered vessels before they allowed troops aboard.

Many of the German ships were renamed. The *Lotheringen*, for example, was renamed the *Moorina*, and the *Germania* became the *Mawatta*. One of these interned vessels had been moored next to *Ascanius* at Port Melbourne the day they left—the *Barambah*.

At tea time on the first day at sea, the men of 'B' Company clambered down the two flights of steep stairs and through the hatchway to their gloomy and windowless quarters. Here, Will carried out his duties as Troop-deck Corporal. That evening the men dined on

---

62   Source: Sea Transport of the AIF. Greville Tregarthen, Naval Transport Branch, (no date). Held at Australian War Memorial Archives.

63   Paterson

cold corned beef, pickles, bread with butter and jam and currant buns for tea, washed down with copious amounts of tea with milk and sugar[64].

Will noted that the mess tables, though laden with such sumptuous fare, were poorly attended. The open ocean was proving to be a bumpy ride. There was a kind of strained expectancy on board, with everyone suspecting everyone else of being seasick.

The men were feeling the effects of the rolling seas. On a similar troopship a year earlier, Captain Charles Arblaster had written that some men had draped themselves miserably over the ship's rail, waiting 'with their mouths partly open and seemed quite disappointed when nothing came [up][65].' It was apparently contagious—seeing one man sick made the others feel ill. No doubt the men would have chaffed each other, those who seemed to be inexplicably immune to sea-sickness talking loudly about fried pork chops and other fatty foods. Will was fortunate in that he rarely suffered from 'mal de mer'.

Supper that evening consisted of biscuits with butter and cheese. Afterwards, when Will had helped ensure that the troop-deck was clean and shipshape, he sat down at the mess table to write in his diary and compose some letters. The seas being rough, he must have been hard put to keep a steady hand.

It had been a long day and the men were looking forward to sleep.

Blackburn:

> About 8.30 we went to bed and great fun was caused slinging hammocks. Each man has about 3 feet or less. Fellows were getting in one side and slipping out the other side. Then when they got in they started swinging. Then we (the ship) got a steady roll, but it did not interfere with our sleep and we slept fine.

---

64   Source: Sea Transport of the AIF. Greville Tregarthen, Naval Transport Branch, (no date). Held at Australian War Memorial Archives.

65   Source: The records of Captain Charles Arblaster, 8th Light Horse, aboard A16 Star of Victoria 1915.

Learning to handle the canvas hammocks caused great hilarity. Would-be occupants had to stand on the mess table to unfasten their beds from two hooks on either side. Each man had about three feet of space to himself, or even less. They were jammed together like sardines in a tin! Men were toppling and whooping all over the troop deck, grinning and laughing and enjoying the fun; hamming it up with pratfalls. Like his comrades, Will must have found the absurdity of the situation supremely comical.

Imagine: As soon as Will is securely ensconced in his hammock, he takes out the little locket containing the photographs of his parents and opens it. He gazes at their dear faces for a while before closing the two halves together and replacing the precious memento in the protective case his mother made. He whispers a prayer, then lies on his back staring up at the grille-like ceiling of 'C' troop deck. This is in fact the floor of the troop deck above. Its open design is intended to provide ventilation to the dungeons below.

Presently, Will closes his eyes and falls asleep. The ship rocks like a cradle. Not even the sounds of men snoring, vomiting, or even falling out of hammocks can disturb his deep slumber.

T.S.S Ascanius
June 5th 1916.

Dearest Mother & Dad,

Today is Monday, the 9th day of our voyage, and the first really pleasant one so far. Since leaving Melbourne we have been going on ever on, without a stop with only the limitless sea on our furthest horizon. And the weather up to this morning has not been too cheerful. The first few days especially were about as bad as could possibly be for the commencement of a sea trip. Heavy seas, cloudy skies, no sun, and a cold keen wind. The water was continually coming overboard, sometimes in rapid drenching spray, at other times in solid douches. Tuesday night was the worst of all. Let me first explain that the troopdeck I am in is situated in the forward hatch two floors below the well deck, therefore really below the water-line. Moreover it's a case of sardines and no mistake. When those hammocks are all slung at night there isn't enough room for a cat to crawl through. Two hatchways give entrance

Letter from Will to his parents, written aboard HMAT Ascanius, 5th June 1916

'On Active Service with the Australian Imperial Forces'

T.S.S. Ascanius, June 5th, 1916.

Dearest Mother & Dad,

Today is Monday the 9th day of our voyage, and the first really pleasant one so far. Since leaving Melbourne we have been going on ever on, without a stop with only the limitless sea on our furthest horizon. And the weather up to this morning has not been too cheerful. The first few days especially were about as bad as could possibly be for the commencement of a sea trip. Heavy seas, cloudy skies, no sun, and a cold keen wind. The water kept continually coming overboard, sometimes in rapid drenching spray, at other times in solid douches.

Tuesday night was the worst of all. Let me first explain that the troop deck I am in is situated in the forward hatch two floors below the well deck, therefore really below the water-line. Moreover it's a case of sardines and no mistake. When those hammocks are all slung at night there isn't enough room for a cat to crawl through. Two hatchways give entrance to this place of a thousand delights and discomforts, wherethrough the visitor after successfully performing the amazing stunt of getting down two sets of steep stairs, will find himself in a dimly lighted enclosure known as "C"' Troopdeck. To prevent this charming hostelry from becoming altogether a black hole of Calcutta the floors of the troop-deck above and the well deck hatch above that are made latticewise, also happily when there are not too many seas about and the wind isn't howling like a pack of mad dogs, a canvas ventilator is let down which doubtless does good work as an atmospheric sewer.

However to proceed about Tuesday night. The wind was howling nice and friendly like and the spray coming over in nice soaking quantities all over the place. For a marvel only two mess orderlies had tumbled down the stairs, hash potatoes, tea and all, to the mild wonder of the unfortunates inhabiting "C" troop-deck. The majority having got sufficiently wet decided to go to bed in good time. Lights were out, hammocks slung, and everyone just dozing nicely about 10.30 pm. when suddenly the storm increased in intensity. Soon huge masses of water could be heard thundering on the well deck. Then a steady drip, drip as the water commenced to soak through the tarpaulin covering the hatchways.

Suddenly a crash louder than usual and then a torrent of cold salty water on the dazed sleepers below. In less time than it takes to think it out the troop-decks were a seething soaking mass of blankets hammocks and bewildered humanity vainly trying to reach some ark of safety from the devastating deluge. Talk about a mess up, you never saw anything like it, not at a jumble sale.

The cause of this sudden catastrophe proved to be a wave stronger than his predecessors which had simply smashed in the port hatchway entrance, thus allowing the water to seethe in freely. I was one of the unlucky ones within range of the incoming waters, but on the first signs of what appeared to be imminent I quickly persuaded myself to tumble out and being ahead of the general pandemonium which broke loose not a minute after, slung my cosy little cot somewhere safely out of range. My boots and some other things I left behind I discovered after some searching the following morning, floating amongst the general wreckage.

This bit of playfulness on the part of Mr Neptune, took some "putting right" as you can imagine. No, life on a transport isn't all beer and skittles. We're too crowded, not enough room for exercise, and alas no room whatever for deck chairs and those comforts which go to take away the monotony of cramped quarters and the unchanging vista of dancing waters.

Weariness brought a halt to Will's letter-writing, followed by four busy days. On Wednesday 7 June the men listened to a lecture on submarine torpedo attacks. The Ascanius was approaching the submarine zone. All the lifeboats and life-rafts were made ready in case of emergency. During the mid-day meal the submarine alarms sounded and the men carried out the drill with great efficiency.

News came by ship's wireless of a tremendous naval battle between the Royal Navy's Grand Fleet and the Imperial German Navy's High Seas Fleet, fought between 31 May and 1 June 1916, in the North Sea near Jutland, Denmark. The two huge fleets, totalling 250 ships between them, were twice heavily engaged. Fourteen British and eleven German ships were sunk at 'The Battle of Jutland', with great loss of life, but it was being hailed as another great British victory. Being at sea themselves, the men of the 39th were deeply interested in all the details.

Not until that evening was Will able to find time to resume writing his letter to his parents.

9.6.16.

As you will see by the above date I am continuing this letter at a later date than I commenced it. Today is Friday and barring a few occasional showers the weather has been all that could be desired. We have now been about a fortnight on the water and are still going strong. I think I told you in a previous letter that I had been made Troopdeck Corporal for the first week of the voyage. I had three different Sergeants to work with and they all turned ill, one after the other. I wasn't sorry by any means when my week was over. It's quite a pleasure to get on deck and away from the oppressiveness of the constant confinement of a troop-deck.

The food on board is particularly good. Now that mal de mer has been got over by all, the boys are developing terrific appetites and as the food is good, well cooked and abundant, the ship represents a fattening pen more than anything else. Of course only a small number of troops are able to exercise at one time on the decks so that the men are by no means overworked. Of course you would like to know where we are going, but this is one of the things the Censor looks upon as his peculiar secret. So you must guess. I might say I haven't seen the Dickersons yet but I hope to do so as soon as I get a chance. Also if I sign myself Palstra you will not be surprised.

We are being enlivened on occasions by such cheerful things as Submarine attack drill, Fire drill etc. To see the fellows scrambling to their posts each with a lifebelt on, is quite an interesting scene. On Sunday we had Church Parade on the Aft Well deck. The men were crowded over every part of the well deck, on top of hatchways, spars and machinery. The Chaplain preached from the Boatdeck. I must try to get a snapshot of the crowd next Sunday. By the bye I wonder if any of the photos I handed you at Port Melbourne came out alright. I quite expect some of them will be spoiled as I hadn't quite got into the way of manipulating the affair [i.e. the camera].

Don't forget to send me a copy of each as soon as possible.

About things to send me: Those dried apricots proved excellent. I put a couple of dozen in a half a cup of cold water and add some sugar at night, and have some delightful stewed fruit the next day for breakfast and tea.

Ditto ditto prunes. So those will be good things to send. Also figs. In short I can see that dried fruit of any kind is always going to be welcome. Before I left you made a suggesting about knitting me small patches to mend my socks with. This will be another good idea. Don't trouble to send large parcels.

Rather send small parcels fairly frequently. Send me a jar of honey as soon as you can, and repeat the dose as often as you think necessary only be careful to pack the jar well. I should say putting the glass jar inside a tin box would be a good idea. At any rate pack it well. Tins of jam & jelly say a tin of quince jelly and a blackberry jam of an extra good kind on occasion would also find much appreciation. Or a tin of tongue (sheep's) etc.

I must say my powers of digestion have become very much better as my general physical state has improved. Nevertheless something extra in the tucker line is one of the little failings of this boy of yours. I think that where we are going we are more likely to receive good food than might elsewhere be the case. I'll tell you one peculiar thing though, I've got so thoroughly to like the Australian method of making tea; the Camp style, boiled with sugar; no milk, that I don't like the tea on board—which is made with the full orthodox ingredients—a bit. Something good for Australia at any rate. The English cooks on board here can lick our Camp cooks with one hand tied behind their backs as we used to say.

There are about six Salvos on board here. I've promised them that if we should get near I.H.Q. [International Headquarters in London, where Will used to work.] I will take them over that historic building, and see if I can't get the General [General Bramwell Booth, son of the founder of The Salvation Army] to shake hands with them. I must try and get them all together on Sunday afternoon if only to read a Chapter together and have a few minutes talk. This place is so crowded it's difficult to do anything like this, but I think it would possibly be a good thing. I'll let you know later how I have managed. Richardson whom I first met out of the six is a very nice fellow indeed. Hails from Hamilton where he was colour Sergt. Is married and has a couple of boys at the front. He's a genuine fellow. None of your blustering blundering blitherers who profess a great deal, ring their own bell a lot and haven't the depth of character of a turkey cock, but a clean living, clean spoken and consistent Christian. He is only a labourer by profession but he is a gentleman in the truest sense of the word for all that, and I often have a chat with him. I like to get these different chaps talking. Later on when I know them all a bit better I will give you some idea of their many peculiarities of character.

Of course I have a Section now. My definite appointment. They are all fine big fellows. I think they are all either as big and bigger than I am bar two, and they are much thicker set than I am. There are fourteen of us altogether. Decent fellows every one of them. I'll have a photo taken of them and send you particulars about each one of them as soon as I can.

It's about 8.45 pm now and we have got the "dinkum oil" or in other words the straight tip that there will be a submarine attack alarm tonight, so everybody is afraid to go to bed lest they have to dress in a hurry. I have my lifebelt handy in case the oil should prove dinkum. Very likely the beggars will wait until lights out—9.15 pm and sound the alarm —one long and two short blasts on the ship's siren about 9.30. That will be a scramble.

We have also got the "oil" that letters for a mail will be collected tomorrow noon so as to give the poor censor some time to get through the huge quantity of correspondence, so I thought I would finish this letter tonight. Once I have seen the Dickersons and we are once more upon the briny I will compile another small budget of information regarding myself. I shall look forward to your first letters. I have a look at my miniature every night before going to bed, and somehow it makes me feel we are not so far apart when I see your faces in the little locket. I am very glad to have it.

And now I shall draw my letter to a close. Very much love to all at home from Het to John not forgetting your dear selves. Don't forget I am looking forward to weekly letters from all of them. I think if they were each to send me something of a letter every mail we could keep up a more regular correspondence. It's a pleasure I should appreciate very much. Of course I know I can expect a letter from you every mail and you can be sure I shan't miss a mail if I can possibly help it.

My letters, at any rate during period of training will be written mostly on Sundays. It's a day when one has time and inclination. You feel so tired often on a weeknight.

Keep cheerful, and believing, the best still lies ahead.

Your loving boy

Will

1916: Voyage Across the World | 2: Shipboard Life

The men of the 39th passed the initial days at sea recovering from the ill effects of sea sickness and settling down to the daily routine of shipboard life. Sick parades were popular and well attended during those early days, whereas the number who turned up at the tables for meals when the bugler sounded 'cookhouse' was remarkably small.[66] The problem was compounded by the fact that many men began to exhibit symptoms of influenza.

During the years 1915 to 1917 'herald wave' outbreaks of influenza were occurring in various parts of the world France, in advance of the pandemic of 1918. Cooped up on crowded troopships the men were exposed to any viral infections that their comrades may unwittingly have carried aboard. Contagious diseases often raged through the entire ship's population, and sometimes proved fatal.

For the men of the 39th, standard army procedure continued at sea as on land. The hour of reveille was six o'clock each morning. Every able-bodied man had to be out of bed and his hammock neatly rolled up and stacked in the bin before breakfast.

Parade took place at nine o'clock, followed by training exercises, known as 'physical jerks' by the men. Most men wore army issue shirts and trousers, a sort of working dress. Officers dressed in more formal attire.

Seven and a half weeks was a long time to keep hundreds of energetic young men confined to a crowded vessel in weather that was sometimes rough, and would be extremely hot when they crossed the equator. Army HQ had mapped out a program to keep the troops occupied.

If conditions were relatively calm, the officers organised drill sessions. Mornings and afternoons were occupied in physical drill, musketry exercises, individual training and lectures on deck, when sea and weather permitted. The large number of troops on board limited the available deck space, and the amount of actual training that took place was correspondingly small.[67]

Ship-board training included rifle drill, bayonet fighting, semaphore, machine gun handling and map reading. The Trumpeter Sergeant sometimes took the buglers on the poop deck for rehearsal, and now and then the officers had pistol practice.[68] Some training sessions involved live firing with rifles and Vickers machine guns.

Paterson wrote that '... deck concerts were frequent when the weather was not too inclement and the 39th Battalion band provided music daily. Music on the sea has a charm and a quality entirely unique, and familiar song and dance tunes played on the swaying decks held their listeners enthralled through long hours of the early days of the voyage.'

'There were three chaplains on board, Paterson recorded. 'On Sundays church parades were held, when the "padres" delivered stirring soldier sermons [chiefly on "morality"] with a hatch as pulpit and the deck for church. There could have been many worse settings for a service than that provided by the deck of the *Ascanius* with the clear canopy of the sky for roof and the strong, clear winds of the ocean sweeping across.'

---

67   Paterson

68   Source: 'Voyages to War: the AIF at Sea.' Doug Hunter, including the records of Trumpeter Sergeant Campbell Rennie, 13th Light Horse, aboard the A34 *Persic* 1915, and the records of Captain Charles Arblaster 8th Light Horse, aboard A16 *Star of Victoria* 1915.

Generally, the evenings were allotted to lectures. Officers and NCOs delivered talks on topics such as 'Squadron in Attack', 'Sentries', 'Orders and Messages in the Field' and 'March Discipline'. The ship's purser gave a series of lectures on 'Map Reading and Field Sketching'. The dentist gave a talk on 'Care of Teeth', and the medical officers spoke about 'Field Dressing of Wounds'. French lessons may also have commenced[69].

Fatigues were numerous. Every day the OC[70] troops and the ship's captain inspected the ship to ensure it had been thoroughly cleaned.

Will must have been pleased when his stint as Troop-deck Corporal came to an end and he was free to spend more time up on deck, out in the open. As a bonus, he was now officially recognised as a substantive corporal (rather than Acting Corporal), and Lieutenant Lenton allotted him his own section. It was a relatively large unit, comprising thirteen men.

By Saturday 3 June 1916, the troops had begun to find their sea legs and become accustomed to their new surroundings. A large number of them were still out of action with influenza, but Will was feeling fit and well, what with the daily exercise, the sea air and the copious amounts of 'good food'.

Every day after a huge breakfast there would be morning tea at eleven o'clock. For dinner at half past twelve there would usually be cold meat and salad but not many fresh vegetables, and plenty of tea. In his book about his war service, Charles Bingham recorded that on his troopship, 'Tea and cake was served at 4 pm—always big slabs of boiled fruit cake, baked on the ship, and dinner in the evening was roast or boiled meat with lots of mashed potatoes. In addition, there was always a lot of chocolate.'[71] This was typical fare.

Paterson wrote, 'Boat drills were ordered often during these first weeks at sea, and practice alarms sounded at many unexpected moments to accustom the men to moving rapidly and without confusion to their life-boat stations. Ocean travelling at this time was accompanied

---

69   Source: The records of Captain Alexander Mitchell, 13th Light Horse, aboard A34 *Persic*, 1915.

70   OC: Officer Commanding

71   Charles Bingham (1st Aust. Casualty Clearing Station 1915 Gallipoli AIF) 'The Boys Who Came Home. Recollections of Gallipoli' by Harvey Broadbent.

by many perils. German raiders were plying their business on the high seas, and the trade routes were never quite safe from lurking submarines.[72]

Paterson recorded that letter-writing filled many of the men's spare hours. The voyagers composed countless long and descriptive epistles and the ship's censors—namely, the senior officers—found their days busily occupied.'[73] All mail had to be censored, in case it contained military secrets that could be intercepted by the enemy or read by enemy spies.

Will had already written one letter home—completed on the day after his departure—and handed it to the officer in charge of mail, to be checked by the censors and posted at the next port of call. He now took some sheets of paper which bore the Melbourne YMCA's elegantly ornate letterhead, and settled down to write a second, longer epistle. Since the rules would not allow him to divulge the ship's destination, he decided to employ a kind of code to let his parents know that Cape Town would be his next port of call. Some Salvation Army friends of the family, the Dickersons, lived in Cape Town. If he mentioned them, Mother and Dad would be sure to take the hint.

Will handed over the letter in an unsealed envelope, so that the censoring officers could look it over.

According to the diary of 'Hughie' Dodd,[74] word started going around the troopships that the senior officers who censored the men's letters laughed at their confidences to their loved ones and made jokes of any terms of endearment.

On learning this, the men called the officers names, and declared they were not worthy of their rank. Will would have heard these rumours. An intensely private person, he may have decided that any future letters he wrote to his family would be less personal and more circumspect.

---

72   'Deck concerts were frequent… lurking submarines.' Quoted from The 39th: The History of the 39th Battalion AIF

73   Paterson, The 39th: The History of the 39th Battalion AIF

74   Source: the Diary of Edward Gilmore Dodd 'Hughie' Dodd, a sapper in No. 6 Tunnelling Company, promoted to Sergeant on the 2nd May, 1916. He embarked from Australia on the 1st June, 1916 aboard the *Warilda*, a ship that was in the same convoy as the *Ascanius*.

1916: Voyage Across the World | 3: Cape Town

Orderlies posted up the wireless (i.e. radio) news on the walls every morning so that the men could learn how the war was progressing and find out about the news from home. The 'Marconi installation'[75] kept men at sea informed of the march of events in the world, and on June 13th there was great jubilation when they received news of the Russian success against the Austrians.

By contrast, only two days later all on board were dismayed by the announcement of Lord Kitchener's death.[76]

Field Marshal Horatio Herbert Kitchener, First Earl Kitchener, was the highest-ranking officer in the British Army, a famous figure whose military career had been phenomenal. His

---

75 A 'Marconi installation' was a 'wireless' telegraphy system. In the early twentieth century the sending of telegrams across the world relied on cables laid across the ocean bed. Guglielmo Marconi, with his 'Wireless Telegraph and Signal Company', developed ship-to-shore cable-free radio communications networks.

commanding countenance, dominated by a huge handlebar moustache, was the focal point of the ubiquitous 'Your Country Needs You' posters. Kitchener had been bound for Russia aboard the armoured cruiser HMS Hampshire when his ship struck a German mine during a force nine gale and sank, west of the Orkney Islands. That such a famous statesman could meet his doom at sea brought home to the troops that the dangers of ocean voyages during wartime were greater than they had supposed. The news cast a gloomy shadow over the ship, and at every meal the discussion was of Kitchener's outstanding career.[77]

Next day (Friday 16 June) the gloom was set aside.

At sunrise, excitement surged throughout the battalion. Reveille had the men tumbling from their hammocks as usual, and when they had clambered up the steep stairs to the weather-deck they gazed out across the waves and saw a dark blue mark on the horizon. Many men were betting on whether it was a cloud or land. As daylight expanded it became clear that the dim outline was the coast of South Africa.

As it was the first land seen since leaving Australia, the sight created quite a stir on board, and men thronged the sides of the ship all day.

At 11 am, within sight of Africa, the ship's chaplains held an impressive 'In Memoriam' service for Lord Kitchener on deck, at the conclusion of which the buglers sounded the 'Last Post'—a soldiers' tribute to 'a great soldier and a great man'.

When the bugler sounded reveille that Sunday morning, the men heard other distant reveilles echoing from inside the harbour. They knew, then that other ships were there besides *Ascanius*. How they cheered and whooped!

They were all up on deck early, before sunrise, lining the rail as the ship waited outside the harbour until it was light enough to enter. The moon, just past the full, shone brightly. At 4 am, in semi darkness, *Ascanius* entered Table Bay at last.[78]

---

77   Blackburn

78   Blackburn

Searchlights swept across the bay and focussed on the *Ascanius* as she steamed towards Cape Town. The distant lights of the city shone out like jewels, and as faint dawnlight glimmered, the vast, fantastic outlines of the mountains looming against the sky could be glimpsed through the morning mist.[79] The men crowding the weather-deck stared at the enchanting spectacle as if they could not get enough of it.

An even more splendid vision awaited them later on, as they neared the docks. Reflected in the harbour, the lights of Capetown looked like some storybook fairyland. Jammed against the rail, the men feasted their eyes on the spectacle.

The first rays of dawn light revealed Table Mountain in all its grandeur and beauty. Mists came swirling down, covering with a white cloth of cloud[80]. It was indeed a magnificent sight. As the ship neared the docks the panorama widened, and the houses of the city could clearly be seen clustering around the base of the mountain. All along the ship's rail men were pointing out objects of interest and calling out to each other. The Cape Town Lighthouse watched over the scene, with its blinking eye.

The waxing light described three large vessels lying at anchor in the harbour—two other Australian troopships, the *Medic* and the *Demosthenes*, and a heavy British battle cruiser with some big guns on board. The name '*HMS Laconia*' was painted on her bows. A vessel of 18,000 tons, she was originally a Cunard ocean liner. Now she was to be the 39th Battalion's guardian escort to 'Blighty'.

A fourth troop transport was expected soon, and on her arrival all the ships, including the *Ascanius*, were to leave port as one convoy.

Will was no stranger to the great continent of Africa. He and his family used to live in Johannesburg, which lay about a thousand miles to the northeast, in the Transvaal[81]. This

---

79   Paterson

80   Paterson.

81   The region used to be called 'The South African Republic', or in Dutch, 'Zuid-Afrikaansche Republiek', often shortened to 'ZAR'. In 1910 the ZAR was renamed 'The Transvaal Province of the Union of South Africa',

was a territory that had been annexed by Britain during the Second Boer War. The official surrender of the Transvaal took place in 1902, the year the Palstra family arrived. Will was then eleven years old.

They lived there for about eight years. Will and his older siblings and went to school at Johannesburg College. It is likely that during his boyhood Will picked up a smattering of Afrikaans—a language derived from seventeenth century Dutch. Most people in Johannesburg—and Cape Town—spoke English.

The men of the 39th, thronging the weather-deck, were eager to get shore leave so that they could take in the sights of Cape Town. As *Ascanius* glided towards her berth they kept their eyes on the slowly approaching shore.

The waterfront was cluttered with a miscellany of skin-drying, wool-processing, fish-smoking, soap making and boat-building establishments. From the foot of the town's main street the new pier, opened in 1913, ran more than three hundred yards out into the harbour. It was crowded with people. A motley and loquacious crowd of people, both black and white in colouring, stood watching the *Ascanius* as she came alongside and made fast. Those of the ship's crew who had visited Cape Town before knew that when word got around that a few shiploads of soldiers with money in their pockets had arrived in the harbour, the locals would come crowding around eagerly.

The only stop-over of the almost eight-week voyage was here at Cape Town, to replenish supplies and coal. The men, who had been cooped up aboard the ship for weeks, were sorely in need of exercise. Lieutenant Colonel Rankine knew that Corporal Palstra had spent his teenage years in that country, could speak Dutch and Afrikaans, and was familiar with the local topography. For these reasons, and because he had proved himself reliable, Rankine selected him to guide the 39th Battalion on the long 'route marches', a task that Will accomplished with flying colours.

The first route march of the 39th in Cape Town, on 18 June 1916, was a memorable experience. The band struck up a brisk marching tune, the drummers pounding out an energetic beat. After passing down the gangway the battalion, followed by the Signal Company, the reinforcements and the tenth Field Ambulance, marched in columns along the wharf and turned into a road running parallel with another wharf. Will, with his lance-corporal at his side, led his section of twelve privates. Ahead of them strode Lieutenant Lenton and the NCOs of 8th platoon. Lieutenant Colonel Rankine, mindful of the exploits of other battalions on shore leave, had equipped the sergeants with notebooks and pencils, ready to take down the name of any man who broke ranks.

The sun was shining as the men looked about, scarcely containing their glee, drinking in every new sight and sound and smell.

Will would have seen similar sights before, during his childhood in Johannesburg, but viewed through his comrades' eyes everything must have seemed fresh and new. The Australians gazed about with delighted curiosity, taking in innumerable brick warehouses, small timber sheds, queues of horse-drawn drays laden with bulging sacks, and chains of goods cars drawn up along the sidings, all overlooked by the harbour's forest of towering masts. Above all, the mighty rampart of Table Mountain climbed into a clear, blue sky.

All the native Africans working on the wharves were clad in European-style clothing. Their garments were ragged, dirty and greasy, but their shirts and trousers covered them from neck to ankle. In startling contrast to their drab garments, their heads were adorned with bright scarves. They waved and grinned at the passing column.

Cobblestone alleyways opened off the main thoroughfare. Small, single-fronted Georgian-style dwellings lined these narrow ways. Their stone walls had been rendered and painted with whitewash, which the years had stained with grime. Front doors opened right onto the street. Large crowds of local children ran alongside the formation of marching men, and fought one another to get near enough to catch the coins the soldiers threw to them, without breaking stride.

Signaller Blackburn wrote of this route march:
> The people treated us fine. They lined the streets, or rather it was an esplanade (probably overlooking the sea), just a Sunday afternoon seaside crowd, and

threw us oranges, apples, cakes of chocolate, cigarettes and handed us books and papers. My word it was a great reception. I've never seen any troops receive such a reception in Melbourne.

The entire scene was buzzing with crowds of dark-skinned people wearing colourful headscarves, who, on hearing the noise of the band and catching sight of the soldiers, erupted into a frenzy of excitement. They rushed up to stare at the newcomers, calling out and gesticulating. Their foreign-sounding words were barely intelligible above the general hubbub.

In the second half of the 19th century the discovery of diamonds and gold had brought a flood of new immigrants to South Africa. Cape Town was transformed into a major port. It was rather a cosmopolitan place, especially compared to Melbourne!

The hundreds of thousands of immigrants included Jews, Indians, Africans, Germans, Italians, South Americans and Portuguese. Paterson wrote,

To the men of the 39th, the Cape Town natives looked a strange, polyglot people. Every type and every colour under the sun could be seen in the streets, their faces varying from pale mustard through cinnamon and brown to pitch black. Representatives of several native races had drifted to Cape Town—Hottentots, Basutos, Swazis and Kaffirs, coolies from Natal sugar plantations—here and there the stately figure of a Zulu, standing out vividly among the rest by reason of his magnificent physique. Score of little half-clad 'piccaninnies' ran about the streets. These blacks, selling fruit, chocolate and cigarettes, ran alongside the marching ranks, and amid much chaff from the 'diggers', succeeded in disposing of their stock at prices which were often ruinously high.[82]

---

82   Quoted from Paterson

This first view of Cape Town created lasting good impressions on the Australian troops, due chiefly to the extreme cordiality which marked their reception by the people of the city.

Having marched for an hour, the men halted in a well-to-do suburb, divested themselves of their heavy packs and sat down in any patch of shade they could find to take a rest and a drink of water from their bottles. Some of them lit cigarettes. The local residents emerged from their fine homes, handing out more fruit and gifts to the troops. Some gave them books, cups of tea, beer, and cake.

At length the men shrugged on their backpacks, the members of the band hoisted up their instruments, and the battalion left the esplanade. The long procession marched back towards the harbour.

'We got back to the ship foot-sore and tired,' wrote Blackburn, probably summing up the opinions of everyone, 'though we had only gone a few miles. After being cramped up on a boat for three weeks it took it out of us, but we were glad. We'd had some fruit, received bundles of books and were delighted with the reception we got from the South Africans.[83']

The excursion had made them all hungry. While the men were away, the Ship's Master had been replenishing the government stores in his charge from the Naval Store Officer in port. Crates of food and extra medical 'comforts' such as ale, pearl barley and arrowroot had been loaded on board, as well as some extra bedding and crockery. Huge hoses filled the ballast space with fresh water.

All provisions, such as dry stores, meats and vegetables supplied to transports had to be examined by government inspectors, who were required to certify that the goods supplied were all of first quality. In addition, all provisions delivered at the ship's side were carefully

---

83   'The Voyage of the 39th Battalion 10th Infantry Bde on the HMAT 'Ascanius' A11 to 'Somewhere' on Active Service,' by L/Cpl Clive Blackburn, Regimental Signal Sect. No. 257, 27th May 1916

checked with the orders given, to ensure that an ample supply was placed aboard to maintain the victualling scale for the whole voyage.

The following day, 19 June, the men of the *Ascanius* rose early to go on another route march. Though it was 8:30 when they fell in on deck, it was after 10:00 am before they left their assembly point on the pier. As Blackburn remarked, it was no easy task to unload a troopship of around 2,000 men. As before, Will was the battalion guide.

The work of coaling continued through that night. The din of the winches and the ceaseless chatter and shouting of the native workmen as the bunkers were being filled made sleep almost impossible. Choked with coal dust, kept awake by constant noise, the men endured a miserable night.

On the morning of Wednesday 21 June, another Australian troopship made port that morning—the *Warilda*. She was the last ship to join the convoy, which was now complete. At eight o'clock she put into the wharf, to cheers from the men aboard the other vessels. Her troops disembarked, assembled in formation and disappeared on a route march at around half past ten.

Shortly thereafter, the passengers of the *Ascanius* did likewise.

Afterwards, for the last time, the 39th marched back through the city, accompanied by the stirring music of the indefatigable band. Further on, some Australian soldiers lined the paths. They were from the *Medic,* and had been given a few hours' leave ashore after lying out in the bay for five days.

Old friends recognised each other, to their mutual delight. For a while, a few men from the Medic marched alongside their mates. They only had time to exchange a few words, but those few words and the firm hand-grip of dear friends were, in the understated words of Clive Blackburn, 'Just great.' Eventually the Medic troops had to leave the column, which passed out of the town back to the boat for the last time.'[84]

---

84   Blackburn

The *Warilda's* troops, also on a route march, had already returned to their ship at 12.45. By then, the Royal Navy was loading guns on all four transports. Anti-submarine guns were mounted on the weather-decks. The next leg of the voyage would be far more dangerous, as the convoy would be travelling through the submarine zone.

The 39th was on board again by 3.30 pm, and an hour later the *Ascanius* cast off her mooring ropes. She moved out of the docks amidst cheers from the men aboard the other troopships, and from the flag-waving civilians crowding the wharf. The battalion's own band played, and all the men sang 'Old Lang Syne', but as Blackburn wrote, the departure brought up memories of Port Melbourne too vivid to make them happy.

The ship moved out into the bay to join the small fleet of Australian troopships, and dropped anchor alongside the Demosthenes, ready to begin the last leg of the voyage in the morning.

Part VII
1916: To England's Shores

1916: To England's Shores | 1 Crossing the Equator

The Mother call'd, and they heard, | Her children over the foam;

The Mother spake but a word, | And the word that she spake was "Home!"

And they answer'd, "Mother, we come!" | And, swift as the homing bird

Gathers wheeling in autumn skies, | High hearts uplifted and stirr'd,

They rose, as the hurricanes rise, | With a lightning of clarion replies.

With the armour of freedom they gird | Them to war: from Canadian snows,

Out of uttermost Ind, and a third | Where the Austral acacia blows,

They muster to smite his foes.

Thro' the thunder of oceans they came: | They sprang to her bugle's call

Young warriors who sought not fame, | But only to render their all

For the Homeland; to fight and to fall.

They fronted the storm and the flame, | They laugh'd in Death's face as they fell!

They rejoiced in red strife, as a game: | They sang as they strode into hell!

With thy race, Mother, is it not well? [85]

---

[85] 'The Mother and her Sons', by Charles Edward Byles, March, 1916

Punctually at 7.30 am on the morning of Thursday 22 June, the armoured escort ship *HMS Laconia* steamed out of Table Bay, followed by the four Australian transports *Medic, Demosthenes, Warilda* and *Ascanius*. *Ascanius* was positioned last because she carried a gun at her stern. The shores were shrouded in mist, and the convoy crept out to sea unseen.

When the mist cleared, Will and his comrades beheld the fine sight of the five ships of the convoy all steaming along together, about two hundred yards apart, their smoke standing up like pillars of cloud.

On leaving Table Bay the convoy entered Atlantic waters, and the risk of an attack from enemy craft increased. From now on, more stringent precautions, which the ship's guard had orders to enforce, would be observed. Lights on deck were strictly forbidden. Deadlights, which were round, metal covers used to protect the ship's portholes in stormy weather, were fastened on in the evenings. Through the hours of night the convoy would follow its course silently and in total darkness. If anyone wanted to smoke at night they were not permitted to do so on the weather-deck and must go down to the lower, windowless decks. It would be considered a serious crime to show a light of any kind.

Ascanius and her convoy, all in position, continued to steam across the ocean beneath blazing skies. Sporting events were held on the decks of the *Ascanius* during the day. Due to the high temperatures, many of them involved water. Corporal Ivor Alexander Williams of the 21st Battalion AIF, aboard the transport *Ulysses*, had passed through those tropical latitudes in June, 1915. He wrote in his diary,

> It is absolutely cruel now, the heat I mean, the perspiration simply pours off one. You put on a clean singlet in the morning and in about an hour's time it is wet through. This brings on prickly heat, which I as usual have rather badly. We had a few boxing bouts in the evening [when sunset brought relief from the heat, and it became cool enough].
>
> The sun is now directly overhead and at mid-day your shadow is about your feet. Had sport again today. Reg and I entered for the Siamese race [on the deck] and pillow fighting on the spar [above a canvas pool filled with

seawater]. We came to grief in the race as we got out of step. I got into the second round and Reg into the third of the pillow fight. In the evening we had a variety entertainment on the boat deck. There were some really good artists and all of whom were boys of our two Battalions.

Besides boxing, other sports in which sub-units competed were tug-o-war, pillow fights and cricket. Deck quoits, cards, letter-writing and reading were also popular pastimes. Trumpeter Sergeant Campbell Rennie, 13th Light Horse, aboard Persic in 1915 wrote:

> On Saturday afternoons we had sports on deck, some of which created no small amount of excitement and amusement. The tug of war being always a keen struggle. The pillow fights over a big canvas tank filled with water being particularly amusing. Some of the combatants striking very funny attitudes as they tried to cling to the slippery pole and deliver a knockout blow to their opponents.

Though the ship was so crowded that there was hardly room to move, the health of the troops on *Ascanius* generally remained good throughout the voyage. The influenza germs were still aboard, however, and spreading slowly, and incubating.

As the days passed, the heat increased. Flying fish skimmed the surface of the water all day and at night the phosphorescence of the sea glimmered faintly like liquid fire along the ship's sides. Each evening the sun went down in a gorgeous blaze of colour. Then with almost startling suddenness night would come.[86]

On Saturday 1 July, the convoy crossed the equator.

> The ceremony of Crossing the Line is an initiation rite in the Royal Navy and other navies which commemorates a sailor's first crossing of the equator. Originally the tradition was created as a test for seasoned sailors to ensure their new shipmates were capable of handling long rough times at sea. Sailors who have already crossed the equator are nicknamed (Trusty) Shellbacks,

---

86   Paterson

often referred to as Sons of Neptune; those who have not are nicknamed (Slimy) 'Pollywogs'. The uninitiated must endure indignities at the hands of the shellbacks before being accepted into their number. [87]

Crossing the Line is nearly as old as seafaring itself. Sailors of antiquity engaged in similar rituals. The ceremony is elaborate, involving costumes and moderate physical violence. Ceremonies in the seventeenth century involved quite severe abuse.

The time-honoured deep-sea ceremony was not observed aboard the *Ascanius*. The officers would not permit the boisterous ceremony because of the chaos it could cause among hundreds of bored, high-spirited young men. They had learned this lesson from past experience.

On Sunday 2 July, the first and only death in the convoy took place on the troopship *Medic*. At about 8:00 pm all ships stopped their engines and hove to, as a burial service was held on the *Medic's* deck and the body of an Australian artilleryman was laid to rest in the deep waters of the Gulf of Guinea.[88]

The burial at sea was a deeply moving event. A jutting board was attached to the side of the ship, on which rested the body, sewn in canvas, weighted and covered with the Union Flag, its bright red and white stripes contrasting with its blue background. The entire battalion assembled on the weather-deck. The parade was called to attention and a chaplain read out the burial service with prayers. The engines slowed as the plank was tilted and the corpse slid overboard, disappearing from view beneath the waves.

A bugler sounded the Last Post and a rifleman fired three final volleys, with a short drum roll between each one. In conclusion, the band played the regimental march as the men returned to parade decks. The engines picked up speed, the ship resumed her journey

---

87   Wikipedia: 'Line-crossing ceremony' retrieved 7th September 2023.

88   'July 2. Buried one man off the Medic at 8 pm (Sunday),' wrote Australian soldier Hughie Dodd aboard the *Warilda*. Disparaging the authorities he added, 'Engines of this ship slowed down for a few seconds only.'

and life went on—apparently—as usual. There was less laughing and joking aboard, and a solemn air reigned.

The Marconi wireless continued to keep the convoy in touch with news of the far-off war. On 1 July,[89] at the same time as the *Ascanius* had been crossing the equator, the Battle of the Somme had commenced in France. The thunder of the barrages was so loud that it could be heard as far away as Hampstead Heath in London. This was to be the British Army's 'big push' that, in the opinion of the War Office, would bring about a decisive victory.

To preserve morale among the troops, the War Office diluted and polished the reports from the front. The full story was not released and the world would not know the whole truth until months or even years later. 1 July 1916 proved to be the most bloody in British military history and the bloodiest single day for any nation in the entire war. Nineteen thousand British troops and an estimated 7,000 Germans lost their lives on that day. Of the 140,000 British, Commonwealth and French troops who went into the attack, almost 60,000 were killed, wounded or missing by day's end—for little territorial and no tactical gain. Putting a positive spin on events, reporters called The Somme a 'stirring battle' and a 'baptism of fire'. When the news reached the *Ascanius* by wireless, the men aboard were cheered and inspired by the feats of their British counterparts.

On 4 July, two days after the burial at sea, the 39th awoke to the startling news that no-one was allowed up on the weather-deck that day. At breakfast time the mess tables were buzzing with rumour and speculation. Overnight, while they slept, something big had happened; on receiving wireless news from another ship in the vicinity, the convoy had extinguished all lights and accelerated 'full speed ahead'. Rumours were circulating that an enemy raider was abroad in the surrounding waters, that the convoy had been 'chased by a German radar' and that their armed escort, Laconia, had been firing her guns. Even more extravagant stories began surfacing as the morning wore on.

---

89   On 19 July, Australian troops on the western front attacked the German-held town of Fromelles as part of the Battle of the Somme, with shocking casualties. This fact was hushed up by the authorities at the time.

Blackburn wrote,

> Tuesday 4th July. Great "furphys" [tall tales] were going around about being chased by a German radar and that our escort had been in action and I don't know what else. The facts of the case were that we got wireless news of a NZ merchant man [ship] being chased by a radar but the radar blocked all communication by "chipping in". Our boats did not stop but went for their lives, all lights extinguished. The only indication today of anything being wrong is no-one is allowed on boat deck so as not to interrupt the wireless.
> All this happened while we were in the land of dreams.

By 'radar', Blackburn probably meant 'sonar', and by 'chased by a radar' he meant 'pursued by the enemy craft'. Radar was not widely used in 1916, so most people did not really know what it was. Sonar, however, was in widespread use aboard ships, especially after 1912 when the *RMS Titanic* collided with an iceberg and sank.

For the rest of the day the utmost watchfulness was observed on every ship, but the voyage proceeded without any abnormal event to mar its tranquillity. The ship steamed on under the glaring tropical sun, across an ocean that seemed to dance with sparks of white-hot metal.

Suddenly there was a stir on the deck. A chorus of doleful singing could be heard, growing louder. Everyone craned their necks in the direction of the sounds. A column of soldiers was marching slowly along. In their midst eight men were bearing, high on their shoulders, a stretcher, upon which a figure lay wrapped in a shroud.

The men were holding a mock burial.

Indeed, the item on that stretcher was the tainted food the cooks discovered the day before, when they were preparing dinner. Several of the onlookers jumped up and joined the procession. The soldiers marched around the ship exhibiting the 'corpse' on high, after which they solemnly lowered it overboard to the accompaniment of hymns chanted by the assembled men.[90]

This was the men's way of dealing with tragedy through humour; perhaps a way of helping them cope with the loss of their comrade on the *Medic*, a young man whom perhaps none of them had known personally, but who could have been any one of them, lying alone now at the bottom of the sea.

Mindful of putting a positive spin on all the army's efforts, Captain Paterson wrote in 'The 39th'—'Apart from this one instance, the food for all ranks is exceedingly good.'

---

90 Paterson

1916: To England's Shores | 2: The Cape Verde Islands and Beyond

The Brisbane Courier (Queensland: 1864 - 1933)

Tuesday 11 July 1916 Page 7

THE SALVATION ARMY.

In addition to the tens of thousands of members of The Salvation Army serving with the Forces, a considerable number of permanent officers of the organisation from Australia have gone to the Front and, according to the latest gazette, two of the latter have received commissions. Private Charles Palstra, son of 'Colonel' Palstra, chief secretary of The Salvation Army, who landed at Gallipoli during the early days of the campaign there, has been promoted to the rank of lieutenant, and Sergeant Judd, another Salvation army officer, has also received this distinction.

On Thursday 6 July, at first light, the convoy sighted land—the first of the Cape Verde islands. A rugged peak rose through the early morning mist; the summit of Jago, an extinct volcano 8,500 feet high.

At 6.30 am on Friday 7 July, the convoy dropped anchor in the Port of St Vincent, the harbour of the Portuguese colony of Cape Verde. Will and his comrades were up on deck with the rest, eager to see the sights. Leaning on the rail, they saw many ships at anchor, including three British cruisers and some German vessels that had been interned by the Portuguese authorities.

Quarantine was in force, and no one was permitted shore leave, but native men paddled out from shore in a small fleet of outrigger canoes and quickly surrounded the troopships. Their boats were full of a variety of goods, their main stock being fruit. On account of the severe heat, the soldiers especially relished juicy fruits such as oranges and coconuts. The enterprising vendors, who were not allowed on the steamship, sold their produce to the soldiers by way of baskets, in which the articles purchased were hauled up to the deck. Some of the soldiers placed coins in billy-cans, which they lowered through a porthole before drawing them up full of fruit. A couple of men lost their money, while others received the goods they had paid for.

The vendors had the advantage of their customers—being down on the water in small boats they were too far away to be bargained with, so the troops just had to take what they could. All day the natives did a roaring trade in beads, shells, bags, cigarettes, fruit etc. and the soldiers of the 39th were eager to get them. The Australians, none of whom spoke Portuguese, had to communicate as best they could with the vendors, who did not speak English.

All were astonished when the Cape Verdeans started catching fish by the hundred. They would chew up a morsel of meat and spit it out in the water, whereupon great shoals came swarming in. Then they would merely dip a hand-net into the water and bail out fish by the half dozens, just as if they were bailing water. Many of the troops purchased fishing lines at exorbitant prices and commenced to angle enthusiastically over the side of the ship.

Soon the weather-deck of the *Ascanius* was crowded from rail to rail. All along one side of the ship fellows were fishing, while along the other side they were buying—or, as they ruefully acknowledged, 'being rooked' (cheated). The harbour was full of fish, and many good hauls were recorded. The men were forbidden to swim, however, because, (notwithstanding the fact that crowds of native men were nonchalantly diving), the water was said to be 'infested with sharks.'

Next morning, Saturday 8 July, native diving boys provided much entertainment for the soldiers while reaping an abundant financial harvest for themselves. Stark naked, they rowed their canoes out to the ships again and performed numerous skilful tricks. They were expert divers, and if the men threw a coin overboard they would plunge in and grab it before it sank.

Will, as a mere corporal was confined to the ship with the rest, but some of the senior officers went ashore. The scanty garments of the islanders led some of them to believe that St Vincent must be 'a most immoral place!'[91]

At last, at 12.45 pm on Sunday 9 July after the usual church parades, the convoy left St Vincent and entered on the third and final stage of its voyage.

The crews of the British warships *Ophir* and *Kent* manned their decks and 'cheered ship' as the Australian troopships steamed out, led by the armed merchant cruiser *HMS Laconia*, with *Ascanius* bringing up the rear. 'A warm-hearted and typically British way the navy has of expressing its feelings!' rejoiced Captain Paterson.

The warm glow of being cheered as heroes soon faded, however. The 39th had now embarked on the most dangerous leg of their voyage, for perilous waters were near, and they were drawing ever closer to the English Channel.

---

91   'Voyages to War: The AIF at Sea' by Doug Hunter.

The *Ascanius* and her convoy sailed on. Before sunset all the lights aboard the troopships were turned off, although the surroundings were still nearly as light as day. Smoking on the upper decks continued to be forbidden, as the flare of a match could attract the enemy's attention.

From this morning until the end of the trip there was increased danger of enemy submarines. This was the most critical period of the whole voyage, a real danger zone, which is why yet greater precautions against disaster had to be observed.

Guards and look-outs were doubled, and the guns of the escorting cruiser covered every passing vessel until her identity and good intentions had been established by means of wireless communication and signal flags.

A special armed 'submarine guard' guard of eighty men (another report said 60) was posted on the weather-deck, with rifles and five rounds of ammunition, to keep a look out for periscopes of submarines or floating mines.[92]

Every hour brought the 39th into more dangerous waters. Lookouts were alert and everyone was on edge. When, on the following day, they passed a Dutch boat, *Thuban*, the battle-cruiser *Laconia* 'came alive', manning all her guns and training them on the foreign vessel.

They entered the Bay of Biscay during the morning of Sunday 16 July. Due to security concerns, no church parade was held on the decks. The men were given a 'marching order parade' at which they received their instructions regarding the landing. Webbing equipment was handed out and officers conducted a full dress inspection. After the inspection the men had to scrub out every inch of the troop decks—floors, walls and fittings.

The first hints of England were the seagulls' cries.

Wistful and strange, the calls of the herring gulls sounded to the ears of the Australians, and melodious by comparison with the strident screams of the southern hemisphere's silver gulls. Perhaps it came to them, then, that they were ten thousand miles away from home.

---

92   Sidney B Young

At 4 o'clock on Monday morning, 17 July, Clive Blackburn and the other signallers were awake and up on the weather-deck. It was their job to decode all the incoming messages, so they knew what was about to happen; they were approaching England's shores, and about to be met by the coastguard.

A thick fog rendered almost all of the other ships invisible. The grey haze muffled all noise except the deep thrumming of the engines and the sound of water lapping at the hull. The men who remained sleeping in their hammocks below decks, unaware of the fog, were almost frightened out of their wits when the *Laconia* sounded her fog-siren.

At 5:30 the low, streamlined outlines of four grim-looking British destroyers came gliding out of the fog. Long, grey guns raked from their decks and smoke pumped from their funnels, dense and dark.

The destroyers took up position, one in front of each transport. By now the troops were crowding the rails, cheering and waving to the sailors, who waved back. The Australians exchanged comments like, 'We're safe from submarines with those greyhounds guarding us,' and 'Good old British Navy!'

With this additional protection the *Ascanius* proceeded towards her destination.

As soon as dawn broke on the morning of Tuesday, 18 July, the men were up and about, all excitement. At half past seven the rocks of Land's End loomed dimly through the Channel fog. The Australians lined the sides of every ship, eager for their first glimpse of England.

1916: To England's Shores | 3: Arrival in England

England, England, England,

Girdled by ocean and skies,

And the power of a world, and the heart of a race,

And a hope that never dies...

And whatever the people that dwell beneath,

Or whatever the alien tongue,

Over the freedom and peace of the world

Is the flag of England flung.

Till the last great freedom is found,

And the last great truth be taught,

Till the last great deed be done

And the last great battle is fought ;

Till the last great fighter is slain in the last great fight

And the war-wolf is dead in his den,

England, breeder of hope and valour and might,

Iron mother of men.[93]

At this time, Will ceased to write in his diary for two weeks. It is a mystery why this happened—the surviving letters give us no clues. Perhaps he was busy with the task of helping set up Headquarters for the 39th, but it is more likely that Will had awoken on 18 July feeling unwell. Measles, influenza and mumps were rife aboard the convoy ships, and it is noted in the official records that several men of the 39th did suffer from the measles during their first days at training camp in England.

The 39th Battalion disembarked at Devonport on Tuesday, 18 July, and boarded long steam-trains that carried them through the English countryside.

Devon in summer, with its hedges and lanes, its trim fields and its pretty, quaint villages, was like a picture postcard. It made a profound impression upon the Australians. Crowded together in their compartments, they leaned from the carriage windows, gazing with appreciative eyes at the changing panorama of wooded valleys and purple moors.

Great, spreading oaks and beeches, and green meadows bordered with hedgerows spread out on either side of the railway line. The wheat harvest was lying in the fields, being gathered in by hand, with people loading the sheaves onto ox carts.

This was an eye-opener for most of the Australians, who had grown up in a landscape of dry paddocks and grey-green eucalyptus trees.

39th Battalion Signaller Clive Blackburn was as enthralled with the scenery as the rest:

> Our train whirled us through cities and typical English villages with stone churches and graveyards. All along the line the people waved. They could not have known we were Australian, so it must be a usual thing to do. At any rate, the English people we saw are extremely patriotic.

---

93   William Wilfred Campbell, (1858?-1918)

Private Norman Thomas, an Australian soldier who would complete that same journey in September 1916 wrote that he and his comrades—

> Had five hours of journeying through scenery that seemed like heaven on earth. Well, it was wonderful—England was at her best. The farmers were harvesting, and in some places fresh crops were coming up. Of course you know the hedgerows that cut up the land and are quite enchanting.

The 39th Battalion's Captain Paterson felt certain that the men would never forget the beauty of that English summer—the last summer many of them would ever know.

As the troop trains passed slowly through local railway stations, women lining the platforms cheered them, and some gave newspapers into the men's outstretched hands.

At the town of Exeter the trains stopped for a short time. Here refreshments—provided by and served by the Lady Mayoress's Committee—were ready for the hungry men. Officers stepped onto the platform of Exeter Station, accompanied by two men from each compartment, whose job it was to collect the refreshments for their fellow passengers.

Wrote Sidney B. Young,

> At Exeter Station a committee of ladies handed us tea and cake and a card with the Compliments of the Mayoress of Exeter. This was very acceptable. The people here seem to be very open and trusting even to the extent of leaving a change counter in a remote corner for 10 minutes surrounded by soldiers.[94]

Each of the officers also received the calling card of the Lady Mayoress. She and her band of volunteers were a hard-working, dedicated bunch. Each day, about twelve troop trains passed through Exeter Station, and since the outset of the war they had looked after every train the same way.

From Exeter the 39th Battalion journeyed on without stopping, north-east towards the county of Wiltshire and into the twilight. Across the sweeping expanse of Dartmoor rattled the trains. Darkness made it impossible to see anything more of the countryside apart from

---

94 Sidney B. Young war diary

the lights of towns and villages. Many of the men dozed in their seats, their heads slumped on their chests.

At about 11.15 pm the battalion arrived in the city of Salisbury. From there, trains carried them to Amesbury, a little village off the London line. Amesbury station was the nearest station to Salisbury Plain. It was brilliantly illumined with electric light and gas flares, making it very easy for the men to 'form up' in marching order.

'Atten—SHUN!' A sergeant bawled out the command, which echoed above the sound of the idling steam engines. 'By the right, quiiiiick—MARCH!'

Night had fallen as the columns began marching along the country roads. After covering a distance of two or three miles, the men reached their billets at the vast, sprawling training camp on Salisbury Plain.

There they lay down gratefully on their beds and instantly fell asleep. As Paterson wrote, 'The fourth phase of the journey had come to an end.'

About eighty miles away from Salisbury Plain, in an office at AIF headquarters in London, an army clerk tapped out these words on a typewriter:

'19th July 1916, Following troops ex 'Ascanius' marched into Camp; –

Headquarters 10th Inf. Bde. (Brig. Gen. W.B. McNicholl)

39th Battalion

1st Reinforcements 10th Machine Gun Co

3rd Divisional Signal Co

Detail of 10th Field Ambulance

1st Reinforcements 39th Battalion

Approx. total 52 officers, 1580 O.R.[95]

---

95 OR: Other ranks

Part VIII
1916: On Salisbury Plain

1916: On Salisbury Plain | 1: The Plain

What have I done for you,

England, my England?

What is there I would not do,

England, my own?[96]

---

96   A.T. Paterson quotes this verse from the poem 'England, My England' (William Ernest Henley. 1849–1903) at the opening of Chapter III, 'On Salisbury Plain' in The 39th: The History of the 39th Battalion AIF. G.W. Green & Sons, Melbourne, 1934. 'England' is used to denote 'Great Britain'.

Troop movements at Amesbury Station. Source: www.warmemorial.org.uk

Located in the south-east corner of the county of Wiltshire between the cities of Salisbury and Devizes, Salisbury Plain is a vast tract of rolling, chalky downlands covering an area of 780 square kilometres (300 square miles). Its soil is spread thinly over soft, white limestone a thousand feet deep, consisting almost entirely of the fossils of minute animals and sea-plants that lived tens of millions of years ago, when the Plain formed the bed of a shallow sea.

Short turf covers the Plain's rolling downs which, before the Great War, were scattered with grazing sheep. There is hardly a tree in sight. The vista is interrupted here and there by the ridge of an earthwork or barrow rearing against the clouds, outlined against a windswept sky.

This is the country surrounding that famous and archaeologically significant circle of megaliths called Stonehenge. It is a landscape of barrows, tumuli, earthworks, hill forts and field systems constructed in pre-historic and early historic times.

To historians and archaeologists the region is the finest open-air museum in the British Isles. To folklorists, Stonehenge is a memorial built by Merlin the wizard of Arthurian sagas, aided by giants, or the burial place of legendary kings. To dreamers it is the enigmatic work of alien beings from beyond the stars.

It was in 1898 that the British Army first conducted exercises on Salisbury Plain. From that time onwards, the Ministry of Defence bought up large areas of land year by year, until it became the largest military training area in Great Britain. As military use of the plain increased, the Ministry constructed new camps and barracks. During the Great War a vast metropolis of huts and tents sprang up, covering what used to be fields and pastures or open downs. An observer described the encampment as a collection of 'tin huts—even the church and the cinema were corrugated iron'. Salisbury Plain was the training ground where British soldiers drilled in preparation for many of the terrible battles fought in Flanders.

And more men, from the other side of the world, now joined them.

In 1916, with the withdrawal of Australian forces from Egypt, AIF base and training depots were relocated to England, along with their counterparts from New Zealand. Various military camps on Salisbury Plain were chosen as sites for the training depots and it was here that battalions such as the 39th did their acclimatisation and final training.

The arrival of the AIF's entire Third Division in England during July 1916 saw the establishment of several large Australian encampments on the Wiltshire Downs, and within a few weeks several military cantonments were garrisoned by Australian soldiers from all five AIF divisions. It was here that the Third Division would train for war on the Western Front, under Australian-born Major-General John Monash. Surrounding the cantonments, the plain stretched away for miles on all sides—great sweeps of gently undulating downs on which men marched, drilled, dug trenches and won imaginary battles all day long.

For soldiers, Salisbury Plain was a country of artillery and small arms ranges, of training areas and dropping zones, of tank tracks and barrack blocks. This was where they learned the art of modern warfare. Located within a couple of miles of the ancient monument of Stonehenge, the military training area covered roughly half of the geological boundaries of the plain.

1916 - 34TH BATTALION ARRIVE IN ENGLAND

WE PASSED THROUGH SALISBURY, AND AFTER A TOTAL RUN OF ABOUT SIX HOURS DETRAINED AT THE LITTLE STATION OF AMESBURY. A THREE-MILES' MARCH IN THE GLOAMING BROUGHT US TO A CITY OF LARGE WOODEN HUTS, WHICH STRETCH IN THEIR THOUSANDS OVER BRITAIN'S GREAT TRAINING GROUND - SALISBURY PLAIN." BY CAPT.-CHAPLAIN A.A. MCCOOK OF MAITLAND, WRITING FROM LARKHILL, SALISBURY PLAINS CAMP, ENGLAND, 9TH MAY, 1916.

Larkhill

The 39th Battalion took up residence at Larkhill, the largest cantonment on Salisbury Plain. It was about six times as big as the Ballarat camp, and except for a few regiments of Englishmen it was filled with Australians and New Zealanders. In fact it was the Australian centre. In Larkhill's huge assortment of offices, dormitories and assorted buildings, the whole of the AIF Third Division was housed, from Divisional HQ (when they arrived), right down the hierarchy to the lowest ranks—about twenty thousand soldiers in all.

Soldiers of 4th Pioneer Battalion, AIF at Stonehenge. 09 Mar 1917. Source: Queensland Museums

Lark Hill Camp on Salisbury Plain circa 1916

Military Camp Huts on Salisbury Plain in 1914 - Photo by Pte John Denholm

Aerial view of military camp huts on Salisbury Plain in February 1917 - AWM C01288

Interior of a mess hut at Lark Hill Camp, decorated for Christmas, December 1916- AWM-C00415

H13935 AWM Larkhill, England. 25 December 1916. AIF soldiers training at Camp 14 as artillery officers, probably for 3rd Division Artillery. The photograph was taken in a Christmas Day light fog. (Donor Captain A.W. McMillan)

Ye Olde Bustard Inn in Shrewton, Salisbury, was popular with Australian soldiers during their time at the military camp. Seen here in 1916, it now operates as tea-rooms, as of 2023. AWM H1 3866

A postcard from picturesque Shrewton, early 20th century.

High Street, Amesbury, circa 1916

On the first morning in camp the men of the battalion—aside from those who were ill—assembled in the mess rooms for breakfast. The food at Larkhill, though plain, was sufficient and palatable and the mess halls were spotlessly clean. The mess room tables were long, and scrubbed daily, while the spacious kitchen was fitted with large stoves.

The 39th Battalion was quartered in Camp No. 7. The two large mess rooms, each adjoined by its own cookhouse and sculleries, were each capable of seating two companies. To the west of the mess halls was a well-stocked dry canteen, as well as recreation rooms containing writing tables, pianos and a supply of periodicals and newspapers from home. There were also a supper room and a drying room. Each camp in Larkhill was equipped in a similar manner, every unit being self-contained and, as Paterson put it, 'not dependent on any other part of the cantonment for anything necessary to the comfort and well-being of its men.'

The huts in which the men were accommodated were comfortable and commodious. Long, wide and spacious, the huts were well lit with electric light, warmed by a stove and ventilated. This was not merely a sleeping place—it was also a living room in which the men could sit comfortably and read, write letters or while away the evenings yarning round the stove. The rooms were furnished with tables and long wooden benches called forms, while the walls were lined with shelves and hooks on which clothing and equipment could be hung, out of the way. Inside the hut each man was allotted 2 feet (about half a meter) of shelf space, and two pegs for hanging equipment and placing clothes upon.

Queensland Times (Ipswich) Monday 24 July 1916 page 4

AUSTRALIANS AT SALISBURY PLAIN, ENGLAND.

A cablegram, under date of London, July 18, states that three of the principal camps at Salisbury Plain have been devoted to the Australian troops. About 40,000 men are spread over the countryside in long, sweeping lines of galvanised iron huts, and in the day-time they drill and manoeuvre on the rolling plains. The men are happy and contented and impressed with the beauty of the country. At night, they have biograph shows and concerts, and the canteens, at which to amuse themselves, and each man is to receive four days leave. The War Office has handed over a commodious barracks for the Australian Headquarters.

LARK HILL CAMP 1916

| Stables | etc |

Regimental Office HQ

| Hut | "D" Coy | | L | I | N | E | S | |

WCs etc   LAVATORIES   etc

| Hut | "C" Coy | | L | I | N | E | S | |

| Writing Room / Supper Room / Dry canteen | Drying Room | Dining Room (500) | | Dining Room (500) | Bath House | Sergeants' Mess |

| Huts | "B" Coy | | L | I | N | E | S | | Quartermaster |

WCs etc   LAVATORIES   etc

| Huts | "A" Coy | | L | I | N | E | S | |

| Officers' Mess | Quarters | |

| Quarters | | |

1916: On Salisbury Plain | 2: Aeroplanes over Stonehenge

On Salisbury Plain, where cloud-shadows raced each other across acres of open grasslands, a man might look up and behold an almost surreal scene. Far off, the stone monoliths of the ancient circle loomed against the skies, while closer at hand a regiment of Light Horsemen galloped by, the plumes of their hats blowing in the breeze. Overhead, a trio of biplanes swooped like giant dragonflies. A single glance could encompass stone-age antiquities, the fading age of chivalry and the dawning era of flight. What a sight it must have been.

One of the most evocative images of the First World War, on the vast expanse of Salisbury Plain, is the vision of fragile, flimsy biplanes wheeling and turning in the cloud-swept skies above Stonehenge; the twentieth century meeting the Paleolithic.

Not only biplanes, with their double wings and criss-crossed struts could be seen swooping and diving above the ancient sarsen stones; tethered observation balloons would sometimes float above the majestic sarsens too. It must have been a surreal, a bizarre, an almost magical scene.

Aircraft constantly patrolled the skies. Probably most of them were from the airfield at Netheravon, about four miles north of Larkhill. As a military camp, Larkhill was a prime target for enemy zeppelins and the British had to remain vigilant. Every day aeroplanes made their appearance, some flying quite low, which enabled the men of the infantry battalions to get a clear view of the whole machine.

Every battalion that marched into camp was presented with the remarkable spectacle of flying machines among the clouds. They were so ubiquitous that the men soon became accustomed to them.

Biplane over Stonehenge, circa 1916. Source: https://airminded.org, 2009

If Will were unwell, then as soon as the battalion arrived at Larkhill he would have asked his sergeant for permission to visit the battalion's medical officer at the clinic. Any tell-tale spots on his face would have proclaimed that he was suffering from measles and after undergoing a rudimentary medical examination with stethoscope and thermometer, he would have been sent straight to quarantine in the infirmary.

He would not have been the only patient! Paterson, as usual playing down the negative and enhancing the positive aspects of the 39th's war experiences, mentioned, 'A slight outbreak of measles which occurred on the second day in Larkhill...'

Perhaps it was while cooped up in the infirmary that he received the letters his parents and siblings had written many weeks ago.

His father wrote in a letter dated 26 June,

> Charley, as you will doubtless know ere this, has got his commission, he was third on the list in the gazette announcement and I am told the position of the names is the indication of the order of seniority of the men concerned...

Will's brother had been promoted to the rank of Second Lieutenant, 6th/46th Battalion on 1 June, just four days after the embarkation of the 39th. This was indeed an increase in fortune for Charles, who was also receiving higher pay for being a returned serviceman. As a subaltern, Charlie was now in a position to command his own platoon, with two sergeants and a batman.

Knowing that such ascension was possible, Will must have yearned to rise higher from his own humble rank of corporal. It seemed that Charlie would always be a step ahead of him, no matter what he did.

Or would he?

Perhaps there was another path, a short-cut . . .

Years later Will would write in his 'War Experiences':

> On the first Sunday morning [23 July] at Larkhill an aeroplane passed low overhead. I had only once before seen an aeroplane and that a long way off. This one captured my imagination, and appealed to my spirit of adventure. I argued also that to be able to fly would be tremendously useful in a country like Australia[97] after the war. There and then I determined I would become a pilot if I could.

The sight of that flying machine altered the course of Will's life once again. It gave birth to the notion that he, an erstwhile office clerk who had seemed destined to live his life behind a desk, might soar through the skies in one of those ultra-modern flying-machines. The idea strongly appealed to him.

It was feasible, too. Many military pilots were deployed purely on reconnaissance work, so there was a good chance that if he got into Britain's Royal Flying Corps (RFC) he could take on a non-combat role that would please his parents and harmonise with Salvationist principles.

What would it be like, to return to Australia as a pilot, with wings on his uniform? How would his family and friends react, when they saw him?

In the popular imagination, aeroplane pilots were considered to be daring knights of the skies, the cream of the armed forces. Immense kudos was attached to the job, in addition to higher pay and numerous privileges. Furthermore, while swooping about among the clouds was undoubtedly dangerous, it would also keep a man out of the equally dangerous filth and degradation of the trenches. There were numerous reasons for a soldier to wish for wings.

Corporal Palstra lost no time. As soon as possible, he made applied for the RFC.

Britain's Royal Flying Corps had only been in existence for four years. It had come a long way in a short time, and now mustered four hundred and twenty-one flying machines,

---

97   "A country like Australia" — a continent of almost three million square miles with remote townships and rough roads. Almost sixty countries the size of England could fit into that area.

with four kite-balloon squadrons and fourteen balloons. By late 1916 pilots were engaging in aerial battles with enemy pilots, as well as the strafing of enemy infantry and emplacements, and the bombing of German airfields.

Australia had an air force too. Of all the British dominions, she was the only one to set up a flying corps for service during the Great War.

Australian pilots began helping Britain in the Great War in 1915. In January 1916 the British War Office made a special request to the Australian government for two hundred volunteers from the AIF to be trained and commissioned as pilots in the RFC. The request, made on the grounds that 'the Australian temperament is specially suited to the flying services', was granted. 183 members of the AIF became officers in the Royal Flying Corps.

Meanwhile Australia's military air unit, No. 1 Squadron AFC, was established in Australia on 1 January 1916. By the time the 39th Battalion arrived on Salisbury Plain, the Australian Flying Corps had not yet entered the European theatre of war. Numerous Australians, however, had already joined the Royal Flying Corps and were stationed in the Middle East. They had sailed from Melbourne in March. The unit arrived at Suez in April and was split into parties for training with RFC units.

An RFC applicant had to be able to read a map and navigate. He also had to have mechanical aptitude and perfect eyesight. Will possessed all the necessary qualities but he still had a problem—he was in the Australian army. He was too late to be among the Australians who had joined the RFC months earlier, on special request. Transfers could be rather difficult and complicated. Many men in Will's position might have given up on the idea, but he was determined to surmount these problems.

'Your application is being considered,' was the non-committal reply whenever he enquired at HQ.

There was intense competition for the glamorous career of aeroplane pilot, and Corporal Will Palstra was one of many hopeful applicants in the queue.

On Wednesday 20 July, a week after arrival at Larkhill, Will was transferred to the Brigade Orderly Room staff. The Orderly Room was actually the brigade's office, the nerve centre of the unit, where the Regimental Sergeant Major and the clerks worked at their desks, dealing with the masses of paper needed for the administration of the large numbers of men and huge quantities of material required to keep the brigade running. Will's superior officers probably selected him not only for his administrative skills, but because he had displayed reliability, resourcefulness and competence.

And so it was that Will found himself behind a typewriter once again, with his clerical skills in high demand. His office duties ran concurrently with his military training.

Sergeant Palstra

Corporal Palstra must have proved his worth in the Brigade Orderly Room, because after a few weeks in this job he was promoted to the rank of sergeant.

He was delighted. 'Sergeant' was the highest non-commissioned rank!

Transfer to the Royal Flying Corps might be a long time coming, and one of the prerequisites was rank, so a promotion was exactly what he had been hoping for. He could never have guessed that his office skills would stand him in such good stead in the army.

If the chance of becoming a pilot seemed slender, other opportunities might be within grasp. Soon after their arrival in England the Australian NCOs were told, 'A few places in the Oxford Cadet Training Battalions will be coming up in the near future. All those who are interested, put your names down. You will be assessed on your performance over the next few weeks, and at the end of that period a small number of you will be chosen.'

Will put down his name as a candidate for a commission. He felt confident he stood a good chance of being selected, and success would further his chances of being accepted into the Royal Flying Corps.

War Horses

Like all the other encampments, Larkhill was crammed with stables and home to hundreds of horses.

Wikipedia tells us that: 'The use of horses in World War I marked a transitional period in the evolution of armed conflict. Cavalry units were initially considered essential offensive elements of a military force, but over the course of the war, the vulnerability of horses to modern machine gun and artillery fire reduced their utility on the battlefield. This paralleled the development of tanks, which would ultimately replace cavalry in shock tactics. While the perceived value of the horse in war changed dramatically, horses still played a significant role throughout the war.[98]'

J M Brereton, the author of 'The Horse in War' wrote: 'the soldier came to regard his horse almost as an extension of his being.' And it is not misty-eyed romanticism to say this, for those at the front had a deep affection for these animals and time and again many memoirs lament the sight of dead or dying horses and mules scattered over the killing ground. It was a case, perhaps of men accepting the nightmare that human hands had created, while feeling that the horrific deaths of defenceless and innocent animals was inherently wrong. Signaller Jim Crow, 110th Brigade, Royal Field Artillery, summed it up: 'We knew what we were there for; them poor devils didn't, did they?'[99]

The Australian cavalrymen did not know it then, but none of their steeds would ever go home. It was too expensive for the animals to be repatriated alongside their owners when the war was over. The men would have to leave their faithful friends among strangers, on foreign shores. Some of them could not bear the possibility of their brave horses being ill-treated. Out of love for their animal companions, instead of leaving them they shot them dead.

---

98   Wikipedia, 'Horses in World War I'. Retrieved 13th August 2020.

99   Source: www.firstworldwar.com/features/forgottenarmy.htm

The 39th did not have any mounted troops—no cavalry, but plenty of horses and mules to haul the heavy equipment[100].

Draught horses and mules[101] would be among the unsung victims of this bloody war. Thousands of defenceless transport animals who were made to drag heavy loads through deep mud under shellfire would be forgotten. They were frightened. They suffered shocking injuries and pain, and they died in their thousands, but there would be no hospital for them, no nurses to bandage their wounds. They best they could hope for was to be shot by the men who brought them into a war that meant nothing to animals, so that death would end their suffering.

Of the 169,000 horses that left Australia for service in the Great War, the only one to return was 'Sandy,' General William Throsby Bridges' (1861-1915) favourite charger.

Work and Leisure

There was never a dull moment for the troops on Salisbury Plain. Evening concerts were arranged from time to time, but the main centres for rest and relaxation were the YMCA huts. Salisbury Plain had several YMCA recreation huts and at least one Salvation Army hut. Sidney B. Young wrote of the YMCA huts, 'The main one is a big, well-equipped building with two billiard tables and different supply stalls where tea & coffee may be had for 1d [one penny] a cup if you don't want cake with it.'

Biggs added, 'In view of the need for haste in the training of the battalion, we work long hours, but a pleasant respite is available in the numerous Y.M.C.A. recreation resorts.'

---

100   Moke: A mule or horse

101   The draught horses and mules would never go home to Australia. If they did survive the war, most would no longer be needed and would be sold to local butchers.

The men also frequented the canteens. Gullet wrote, 'The camp canteens were good, but prices were high, although both in them and at the excellent recreation huts we get a cup of tea and a cake for tuppence.[102] Fresh fruit was in season. Sidney B. Young of the 10th Battalion commented, 'Strawberries are cheap—at the canteen you can get a saucer of strawberries and cream for tuppence, too.'

Despite the joys of cheap cake and strawberries with cream, the men were itching to get out and explore. Biggs of the 40th Battalion wrote, 'About a mile and a half from our camp lie the remains of the famous Stone Henge, which is visited every night by many curious soldiers—and it is well worth a visit.[103]'

Captain Paterson wrote: 'It was not until the ban of quarantine was removed that the men were able to visit the adjacent country. Stonehenge attracted many sightseers. This ancient temple of the Stone Age was quite near to the camp, and in the summer evenings numbers of the men walked over to gaze on the massive stone slabs which had witnessed many ancient rites, and which have so well withstood the wear and tear of countless centuries. A police constable well versed in the history and legends of Stonehenge was always on duty there, and he had a large and interested audience of Australians to listen to his recital of what is known as to the origin and building of this strange temple of prehistoric Britain.'

Whenever the men were given leave, they explored their surroundings. On Sundays they would walk in groups to Stonehenge, or to the quaint local villages which they would explore at leisure. Paterson wrote that in 1916 the villages of Salisbury Plain were among the most beautiful that England could boast. Most of them consisted of groups of tiny thatched cottages half-hidden among spreading oaks and elms. Church towers, centuries old, rose among the trees and on Sunday mornings the bells from a score of these villages sounded

---

102 Gullett Healesville and Yarra Glen Guardian (Vic. : 1900 - 1942) Saturday 25 August 1917 Page 1

103 Signaller Reginald (Reg) A. Biggs (from Tasmania), 40th Battalion Examiner (Launceston, Tas. : 1900 - 1954) Tuesday 17 October 1916, page 7

melodious chimes over the plain.[104] There were cosy local pubs such as the 'Stonehenge Inn' situated just inside Durrington Walls, and the 'Bustard Inn' whose name provoked much merriment and punning. These 'watering holes' were much frequented by off duty soldiers though Will, as a Salvationist, would not have set foot in any of them.

Conceivably on their first day of relative freedom, Corporal Palstra and his friends seized the opportunity of the daylight hours after training to visit the Stonehenge monument. They would have crossed the rutted, dusty road called 'Strangways', which circumscribed Camp No. 7, and struck out south west across the fields surrounding the hutments. The great stones of the ancient monument jutted like broken teeth on the distant skyline.

They were not alone. Men from all battalions were also walking across the grasslands to Stonehenge to do some sightseeing. As the soldiers strode across the wiry turf they would hear, in the distance, the thunderous booms of the artillery firing on the Larkhill ranges. All the roads around Stonehenge carried heavy military traffic and often the rumble of a lorry assailed their ears, or the rattle of a horse-drawn wagon. Closer at hand, the light chirrups of whin-chats and grasshopper warblers emanated from the juniper scrub and low heath. Perhaps a biplane flew low overhead, and perhaps in the direction of Farnborough, faint as a ghost, a sausage-shaped kite balloon was rising into the clouds.

---

104   Paterson

ART03546 AWM Stonehenge, Salisbury Plain 1916 Stonehenge is silhouetted against a sunset sky. The artist, Major Edwin Summerhayes, originally an architect in Perth, Western Australia, served with the 44th Battalion on the Western Front. The 44th Battalion encamped on Salisbury Plain July - November 1916 prior to being sent to the Western Front.

Further off, the brooding megaliths of Stonehenge clustered together like a gathering of grey trolls. The breeze snatched at the coats and hair of the young soldiers as they leaped over tussocks of blowing grass.

At the outskirts of the monument those who had paid their fee joined an audience of British, Australian, New Zealand and Canadian soldiers who were clustered around a British policeman whose job it was to supervise and inform visitors. Amongst the khaki uniforms he looked distinctive in his dark blue outfit. and his domed custodian helmet.

Healesville and Yarra Glen Guardian, Saturday 25 August 1917 page 1

ON SALISBURY PLAIN. The following article, written by Gunner HS Gullett, an Australian journalist serving with the Australian Field Artillery, Australian Imperial Force, has been made available by the Minister of Defence.

Our Men in training

In our own time we can visit villages, or go anywhere else within a 5 mile radius. Special "road" passes are freely granted, and with these we can motor to Salisbury and other large towns further afield. Garages are plentiful about the camps, and fares are not excessive to the Australians, who on all the roads, make dust for consumption by the poor trudging Tommies. . .

Within the camp itself there are many special classes and each day men go off by train to take a course of instruction in gunnery, bombing, machine guns, engineering, fitting and turning, motor mechanism, horse shoeing, and in fifty other crafts and callings directed to the maintenance of our vast army, or the destruction of the enemy. . .

Outside a big camp hospital the other day I saw a group of Australian and Tommy convalescents at play with an improvised switch back railway. They had collected a few hundred yards of old rusted line, built a ramp at one end, with many turns and bumps, and then secured a ricketty truck. They would, after much labour, haul the truck to the top of the ramp, and having tied it fast, all jump aboard. With a shout the rope was pulled and they went laughing excitedly over their bumpy course. Wherever you find him, the Australian soldier is careless of his troubles, gay and simple and wholesome-hearted.

Before many days had passed, the usual military routine was established and the training of the 39th continued from the point where it had ceased at Ballarat. The men were put through bayonet instruction, practice at the rifle ranges, route marches and more. 'Field service schemes' were often carried out, and the difficulties of concealment afforded by the flat nature of the surrounding country assisted the men in learning to take cover.[105] The work was hard and solid.

On the whole, the Australians on Salisbury Plain were warm, well-fed and not unhappy. They seemed as careless of their troubles, as cheerful and high-spirited as if they were not in the middle of the most terrible and bloody war the world had ever known.

Meanwhile on the Front Line

What was happening on the front line at this time?

The First, Second, Fourth and Fifth Divisions of the AIF were fighting and dying in their thousands. Meanwhile, the Third Division had yet to fire a shot in their first battle. The men of the Third were well aware of the attitude of the veteran divisions towards them.

As mentioned earlier, the seeds of resentment had been sown long before, when the Fourth and Fifth Divisions were just being formed. The battle-seasoned soldiers in the new Fourth and Fifth Divisions, which General Birdwood originally named the 'Third' and 'Fourth', were none too pleased that they were forced to give up their titles because the new division formed back in Australia had been named the Third.[106] They were older divisions and they had been in the thick of the fighting. They had seen active service at Gallipoli and in France, but now their names made them out to be behind the Third, who in their opinion were still 'wet behind the ears.'

The men of the Third Division had to put up with some heckling from the old sweats of the four older divisions, but this made them all the more determined that they would soon show them they were 'up to snuff.'

---

105 Examiner (Launceston, Tas. : 1900-1954) Friday 3 November 1916 page 3

106 AWM Records of CEW Bean Chapter XIV – The Flanders Plan. The 3rd Division

They were nicknamed the 'baby division' too, because they were going to be last into the Line, and their men were new recruits, while the troops of the other four divisions were all experienced. In response the men of the Third vowed, 'They'll see. They'll change their tune when we make a name for ourselves in France.'[107]

One of the other epithets for men of the Third Division was the 'eggs-a-cook', because of their oval shoulder-patches. This name derived from the cry of the 'Gyppo' (Egyptian) street vendors in Egypt, where the older divisions had done their training. The Arabs were always selling fruit and chocolates and other foodstuffs, and they advertised their hard-boiled eggs by calling out 'Eggs-a-cook. Verra sweet, verra clean. Two for one'—that is, two eggs for one half-piastre. At Gallipoli the phrase 'eggs-a-cook' was used by the troops as a war-cry when going over the top.[108]

When the Third Division appeared on the scene, with their oval colour patches, some of the fellows in the four 'Fighting Divisions,' as they called themselves, started yelling out, 'There they are. Eggs-a-cook.[109] Verra nice, verra sweet, verra clean. Two for one.' It may have begun as a joke, but it developed into a term of derision.

The Third Division was subjected to a further indignity.

A proud symbol of the Australian Imperial Force was the slouch hat. Australian soldiers wore it with the brim turned up on the left side and secured on that side with the badge.

Having taken command of the Third Australian Division on 1 July 1916, Monash secured approval from General Birdwood for the men to cease wearing the slouch hat like the men of the other divisions. Instead they would wear their hats 'brim down, badge to front'.

---

107   The Third Division would make a name for itself at Messines and Passchendaele, and later on with its greatest exploit of all at Dernancourt, which gained for it unstinted praise and everlasting respect.

108   Source: Gallipoli Slang http://user.online.be/~snelders/slang.html

109   'Oh, the First and the Second are in the line, And the Fourth and Fifth are behind them. But when we look, for the Eggs-a-cook, I'm damned if you can find them...' (This is a genuine ditty of the era.)

It was intended as a mark of distinction, like the ostrich plumes on the hats of the Queensland Mounted Infantry, or the wearing of colour patches on hat bands by the 4th Australian Infantry Brigade. Monash declared that a unique way of wearing their uniforms was a way of making the men of the Third Division bond, and making them feel part of an exceptional group.

The men hated the new style. The most cherished desire of the Third Division's new recruits, as yet untried on the field of war, was to be just 'one of the five'. Surely, if Monash had known how his order as to hat-brims burned in the men's hearts, the brims would have been looped up that same hour.[110]

The 39th battalion was fortunate to be in England during summer. Salisbury Plain turned into a nightmare of mud during the winter months, as the following poem indicates. Note that 'We're not Downhearted' refers to the title and refrain of a song that was popular at the time. This poem was printed on postcards that could be purchased in many camps, with the name of the particular camp inserted in the last verse.

---

110   In late 1917, for reasons of conformity throughout the corps, Monash instructed his division to adopt the same style of wearing the hat as the rest of the Australian forces. (Australian War Memorial).

According to 'Defenders of Australia: The Third Australian Division in WW1': 'To the relief of the men, General William Birdwood reversed this order upon the formation of the Australian Corps.' (Nov 1917)].

The Register, Adelaide, S.A. Saturday 16 December 1916

"A South Australian soldier who recently underwent a course of training at Larkhill Camp has forwarded a poetical description of the place to his father . . .

"LARK HILL CAMP.

There's an isolated, desolated spot I'd like to mention,

Where all you hear, is 'Stand at ease,' 'Slope arms,' 'Quick march,' 'Attention.'

It's miles away from anywhere, by Gad, it is a rum 'un,

A chap lived there for 60 years, and never saw a woman.

There are lots of little huts, all dotted here and there,

For those who have to live inside, I've offered many a prayer.

Inside the huts there's RATS as big as any nanny goat,

Last night a soldier saw one trying on his over coat.

It's sludge up to the eyebrows, you get it in your ear,

But into it you've got to go, without a sign of fear.

And when you've had a bath of sludge, you just set to and groom,

And get cleaned up for next parade, or else's, it's 'Orderly room.'

Week in, week out, from morn till night, with full pack and a rifle,

Like Jack and Jill, you climb the hills, of course that's just a trifle.

'Slope arms,' 'Fix bayonets,' then 'Present,' they fairly put you through it,

And as you stagger to your hut, the sergeant shouts, 'Jump to it.'

With tunics, boots, and puttees off, you quickly get the habit,

You gallop up and down the hills just like a blooming rabbit,

'Heads backward bend,' 'Arms upward stretch,' 'Heels raise,'

Then 'Ranks, change places,'

And later on they make you put your kneecaps where your face is.

Now when this war is over and we've captured Kaiser Billy,

To shoot him would be merciful and absolutely silly.

Just send him down to Lark Hill there among the Rats and Clay,

And I'll bet he won't be long before he droops and fades away.

BUT WE'RE NOT DOWNHEARTED YET.

Throughout September the conscription issue caused deep divisions in Australian society and within Hughes' own governing Australian Labor Party. The controversy at home provoked vigorous debate among the troops, both in camp and at AIF Headquarters where Will was working. Australia was under political pressure to establish conscription because Britain had already introduced it in January, and New Zealand had followed suit in June.

Those in favour argued that more reinforcements were needed on the battlefields, and that the original Anzacs had served their time for their nation and family, whereby it was now the turn of others to do the same for them. They felt that those who were against were no true patriots, and that they were siding with the enemy by refusing to send more Australian troops against them. If Australia expected to receive the support of the British military, the country should not stop helping them in return.

Like his own parents, Will was in favour of conscription. They believed that Australia had a duty to her own men who have already made sacrifices and fought in the War, by not allowing their efforts to be in vain.

People who were against conscription protested that it denied men their basic human right to freedom and was equivalent to forcibly sending a man to his death.

At AIF HQ, as at Larkhill Camp, anti-conscriptionists were in the minority.

In the end, the Australian people voted against conscription. Every Australian who enlisted to fight in the Great War would be a volunteer.

The King's Review

A momentous event took place on 27 September, when none other than His Majesty King George V visited Salisbury Plain to review the Australian and New Zealand troops. As the head of the British Empire the King was the most consequential statesman in the world. The significance of his visit was lost on no one.

That morning, the country roads of Salisbury Plain were full of Australian and New Zealand soldiers marching to the rendezvous at Bulford. Tidworth, Larkhill, Rollestone and all the other camps on the plain sent their quotas, led by the bands of their respective units. Artillery and infantry could be seen moving over the Downs on all sides, towards the place of assembly. The review was held near to the village and camp of Bulford, on an open stretch of meadowland, sheltered along its entire length by pine woods.

On the fringe of the trees an enclosure had been railed off in which stood a flagstaff to mark the saluting base. Along the opposite side of this field the division formed up in line of battalions in column, a great stretch of khaki-clad humanity as far as the eye could see. Behind the railings at the saluting base a large crowd had congregated, among which were many wounded Australian and New Zealand soldiers and nursing sisters from Hospitals on Salisbury Plain. Someone had brought a small kangaroo,[111] evidently a regimental mascot, which caused much amusement among the crowd as it hopped back and forth about the

---

111 They had brought a live kangaroo with them from Australia. This was not a unique occurrence. The 9th and 10th Battalions AIF brought a kangaroo, the regimental mascot, to the Middle East. Many Australian units brought kangaroos and other Australian animals (such as possums) with them to Egypt. Some were given to the Cairo Zoological Gardens when the units went to Gallipoli. (Digger History)

enclosure. The troops sat in little groups on the grass, smoking and yarning contentedly at their ease as they waited, yet ready to be in position at a moment's notice.

Suddenly a bugler sounded a long low note. In less than a minute, officers and enlisted men were in position and stood steadily awaiting events. There was a stir among the assembly at the saluting base, as two motor cars glided up and came to a standstill. A moment's pause, then the great parade presented arms, and the hand of every officer came to the salute as the Royal Standard was unfurled from the flagstaff, and the massed bands burst into the strains of the National Anthem, 'God Save the King'.

He had arrived.

His Majesty King George V, accompanied by his Staff and the Divisional Commander, made his tour of inspection of the parade, after which, mounted on a magnificent black charger, he took the salute as the troops marched past. Led by the batteries of Field Artillery, their guns moving wheel to wheel, the division marched past magnificently. For well over an hour the spectators were held in admiration as the long lines of marching men passed before the King. Overhead an aeroplane patrolled ceaselessly to and fro, seen every now and then amid the rifts in the low clouds.

Will made judicious use of his camera and hoped he had managed to take some acceptable photographs of the proceedings, to send to his parents.

Of this occasion, Major General John Monash wrote: 'As the King rode up to the flagstaff the great Royal standard, which had been coiled up in a ball at the masthead, was broken out and fluttered into the breeze precisely as I gave the Royal Salute, and 27,000 bayonets flashed together into 'Present Arms,' and the 16 massed bands played six bars of the Anthem. It was a moment of glorious sunshine… an impressive and magnificent spectacle.'

Monash wrote about this occasion in a letter to his wife:

> I had the troops drawn up, closely packed together, 100 deep, on the sloping field adjoining the road, and as the King rode by each unit broke into deafening cheer upon cheer, raising hats aloft on bayonets. It was a stirring

sight, and our horses, though terrified, behaved splendidly. The King rode with his head bowed, looking grave and solemn, and when he had passed the last of the troops, he turned to me and said, 'It makes a lump come in my throat to think of all these splendid fellows coming all those many thousands of miles; and what they have come for.' And he said not another word till we reached the station and he dis mounted ...

... I forgot to mention that the first thing he did when he dismounted was to take a lump of sugar out of his pocket and give it to his horse ...

KING GEORGE V REVIEWING HIS TROOPS ON SALISBURY PLAIN, 27TH SEPTEMBER, 1916

In November 1916, as, spring showers flurried from the grey skies above Melbourne and rattled on the window-panes, Will's mother wrote a letter to her eldest son. Its contents indicate he had told her that his application to join the RFC had been refused.

Northcote, Walker Str. 13-11-16

My dear Will,

Hurrah a long letter from you—dated 27-9—reached us yesterday. I have just gone over it again, it is sparkling with energy and life, it was as though I felt it coming into my veins! I got enthusiastic too. However I fear that for the moment they have not given you the chance that was just temptingly held before you, but who knows you may all the same become a flying man. Of course, I would not be your mother if at the same time I did not get a picture before my eyes, seeing you not more than a speck between heaven and earth in all kinds of imaginable dangers.

I suppose all mothers have done the same since their reckless sons explored the depthng [sic] and matches were in fragments over the yard [shattered wooden sticks from home-made flying machines, scattered across suburban gardens].

And now goodbye for this week my dear boy, may the Lord keep and protect you, much love from us all,

your ever loving,
Mother.

The year 1916 waned, and winter arrived in the northern hemisphere.

On the morning of 14 November 1916, Brigade HQ received a divisional memo of enormous significance. The whole of the Third Division was to embark for active service on 21, 22 and 23 November.

This was the goal for which the men had been training for so long. Soon they would confront the enemy and try out their courage under fire. Would they pass the test?

For them, the only kudos that really counted was the kudos of combat. No amount of education, noble blood, wealth or fame could equal the status given, in the army, to a soldier who had fought on the front line.

Great excitement prevailed among the men when they were told to get ready to leave. It must have been a strange feeling, receiving this fateful news. By all accounts the men felt a thrill of elation and excitement, tinged perhaps with incredulity that the longed-for and long-imagined moment was at hand.

Rumour held that it was France they would be bound for, but they were forbidden to mention their probable destination in letters home, and the censors made sure the information did not slip through.

The intervening days were fully occupied in making the final preparations. Steel helmets and gas masks were issued to every man, and on the eve of the departure a hundred and fifty rounds of ammunition per man were issued. Additional issues included a general service blanket, a waterproof ground sheet, an ampoule of iodine, a respirator, a service box, a lanyard, a rifle and a jerkin.[112]

John Monash, Colin's Farm, 21 Nov, 1916.

> The division started to move at 5 o'clock this morning by train to Southampton and thence by ship to Havre and Rouen. It will take 87 railway trains, each of about 30 coaches and trucks, to move the whole division, and the move is spread over six days.
>
> On Friday we had our first snow. The War Office authorities say the division is 'the best equipped division that has ever left England.' Southern Command says it is the best trained division that has left since the old army disappeared.

Snow lay on the ground, and during the last few days of training, the men felt the cold very keenly.[113] Many of the Australians had never seen snow before. On the last Sunday in

---

112   Paterson

113   Paterson

camp they marched through snow four inches deep to Rollestone Rifle Range, where the final Lewis gun practices were fired.[114]

The winter of 1916-17 was shaping up to be one of the coldest on record. Snowstorms covered Salisbury Plain with glinting white powders, and inside the camp huts the men kept the stove-fires continually burning.

The men were constantly hungry for news from the war zone. On 18 November 1916, the Battle of the Somme officially ended. The Australian troops were now garrisoning the front line east of Flers. From there they kept pressure on the Germans by means of small attacks and raids. However, the main battle was now against mud, rain and frost-bite.

On 20 November the first units of the Third Division left for France, marching out of camp amid lusty cheers from their comrades, who were to join them at the front very soon afterwards.[115]

Thursday, 23 November, 1916 witnessed the departure from Salisbury Plain of the 39th Battalion. Paterson records that by the end of the months spent at Larkhill Camp the men had become fit, well-trained soldiers. Their sinews had hardened, he wrote, and the majority declared they had never felt better in their lives. After chafing for months under the routine of drill and exercise, the battalion at last emerged as a smart, well equipped, highly trained fighting unit, with every man fit and eager to get to grips with the enemy. Its strength was two thousand, two hundred.[116]

Reveille was sounded at 4.30am. It was a cold, bleak morning on which they partook of their last breakfast at No. 7 Camp, Larkhill. After the meal, a period of tremendous hustle and bustle ensued. There was strapping and unstrapping of equipment, the packing of packs, to say nothing of the unceasing struggles to get all personal possessions, gear, ammunition,

---

114   Paterson

115   The sick, and those who had been in contact with mumps patients were among those who would be left behind.

116   http://the39th.googlepages.com/themen

rations, blankets and utensils securely buckled to their bodies. These weighed approximately a hundred pounds, exclusive of rifles.

At length they fell in for final inspection then, to the cheers of the few men remaining in camp and the strains of bands playing, off they marched on the four-mile journey to Amesbury railway station, gaily marching to the strains of a popular air such as the 'Colonel Bogie March' played by the Battalion Band.[117]

The following words were written in the autumn of that same year, describing the leaving of reinforcements for France. It is a moving piece, and helps give us an idea of the atmosphere prevailing at such departures.

The Sydney Morning Herald, Wednesday 27 September 1916 page 5

```
A PAGE FOR WOMEN

Leaving Salisbury Plain.

Near Salisbury Camp

I can't tell you how wonderful it is to find oneself living
in a military area. Aeroplanes, with their palpitating hum,
pass continually across the perfect sky, guns boom from
Lark Hill, firing real shells. The tapping of the machine
guns, the marching of troops, the noise of motor bicycles
ridden by earnest looking warriors, and the passing of
military cars, carrying staff officers ("brass hats"), their
red tabs blazing in the sun, break the monotony of each
peaceful summer day.
```

---

117 Digger History.com. the Departure of the 42nd Battalion. On the same day the Fortieth would follow on their heels, tailed by the Eleventh Australian Machine Gun Company, the Eleventh Australian Trench Mortar Battery, the Ninth Australian Field Ambulance, the Tenth Australian Field Company RE, the Z.2.A. Trench Mortar Battery (personnel), the Third Australian Mobile Veterinary Section, HQ & No. One Section Signal Company, and No Three Section DAC. It was the third day of mass embarkations–there would be five such days in all.

```
At first, I could not sleep a wink at night, as all the time
ASC motor lorries were passing on their way, or troops were
marched past — hundreds upon hundreds of Australians and
New Zealanders. The country here overflows with them, and
their behaviour is so splendid. I glow with pride in them
— splendid, brown, dusty fellows.

I was awakened yesterday morning by the noise of a band and
faint cheers, and, dashing to my window, I beheld a sight
I shall never forget — a detachment of Australians off to
the front. The sun was already warm, and they were powdered
with the white dust, but their brave, brown faces were
simply glowing with excitement. Every man was decorated with
poppies and flowers gathered from the fields as they marched.
They were shouting and singing in their excitement, but no
man's eyes carried a fear — one thrilled at the sight.

To the horror of this select hotel I could not remain quiet,
but throw out all the flowers in my room, and shouted "Good
luck" and "Coo-ee." The dear boys were so excited to hear
it — all started coo-eeing, and then began, "Australia will
be there!" and so they sang till they were out of sight.

SOLDIER'S WIFE.
```

Of the day of departure, Captain Paterson would later write in the battalion's official history:

> The spirit pervading the battalion on the eve of going into action is worthy of comment. The men, hardened in physique by the months of strenuous training and resolute in determination to uphold the name of their battalion, were eager to match themselves against the soldiers of the enemy. They were not ignorant of the hardships and trials which awaited them, but these were discounted by the confidence the men had in themselves and in their leaders. It is this spirit which, permeating the ranks of the AIF, has been the foundation of the reputation gained by Australian soldiers in the Great War.

At midday on Thursday, November 23, the battalion left Larkhill and marched for the last time down the road to Amesbury, where three trains were waiting to convey the troops to Southampton.

The quays of Southampton have witnessed many moving scenes in the drama of war. From them the majority of the men of the British armies departed on their way to the battlefields of France and Flanders. From those first tense days of August, 1914, throughout the duration of hostilities, the great pageant of Britain's martial power had passed—for the most part secretly and silently—through the precincts of the town. From these wharfs the first British Army sailed for France—the men who, a few days later, fighting against stupendous odds, were to retreat so stubbornly down the road from Mons. Here again the turbaned regiments of the Indian Army embarked for the front, and now stalwart men of the Australian Forces thronged the quaysides on their way to join their compatriots in arms among the allied armies.

During the afternoon of November 23, 1916, the men of the 39th Battalion sat resting on their piled-up equipment in one of the many large covered sheds beside the Southampton Docks. Alongside the wharf, with steam up and the Blue Peter[118] flying, lay the Admiralty Channel Transport, 'Princess Victoria'.

Embarkation officers hurried busily to and fro among the groups of waiting men, and the crowded dockside presented a scene of great animation. Suddenly, sharp orders rang out and the men rose quickly, donned their equipment, and for the succeeding half hour streamed up the narrow gangway. As each stepped on board he was handed a lifebelt which he had to fasten on, as soon as he had taken off his equipment on the troop deck below.

---

118   Blue Peter: the blue-and-white maritime signal flag hoisted by a ship in port when she is ready to sail.

At 5.30 pm the 'Princess Victoria' cast off from her berth and picked her way out through the crowded shipping into the waters of the Solent, bound for Havre.

The old ordered sequence of camp life with its routine and security was left behind. In a few days the battalion would be plunged into the maelstrom of war with all its horrors, its perils and uncertainties.

It was a grand sight to see all the transports leaving for France, being escorted by destroyers and seaplanes.

Factis Non Verbis, 'Deeds Not Words' was the motto of the 39th Battalion, and now they were about to prove it.

Though the 39th had departed, some of their number were left behind. These included a handful of men who were sick and some others who had been in contact with mumps patients...

... and a few who remained in England for other reasons...

Part IX
1916/17: City of Dreaming Spires

1916/17: City of Dreaming Spires | 1: Oxford

I saw the spires of Oxford | As I was passing by,

The grey spires of Oxford | Against the pearl-gray sky.

My heart was with the Oxford men | Who went abroad to die.

The years go fast in Oxford, | The golden years and gay,

The hoary Colleges look down | On careless boys at play.

But when the bugles sounded war | They put their games away.

They left the peaceful river, | The cricket-field, the quad,

The shaven lawns of Oxford, | To seek a bloody sod—

They gave their merry youth away | For country and for God.

God rest you, happy gentlemen, | Who laid your good lives down,

Who took the khaki and the gun | Instead of cap and gown.

God bring you to a fairer place | Than even Oxford town.[119]

---

119   Winifred M Letts, 'The Spires of Oxford', in A Treasury of War Poetry: British and American Poems of the World War 1914-1917, ed. George Herbert Clarke (Boston and New York: Houghton Mifflin Company, 1917).

On the day of the battalion's departure, Will wrote in his pocket diary–

> 23-11-16 3rd Division leaves for France. I am attached pro tem [for the time being] to 3rd Div. Art. [Artillery] which is remaining behind, having been selected to do an Officers Cadet Battalion at Oxford for a Commission.

Sergeant Palstra's application to study for a commission had been accepted. He had been chosen to undertake a four months' Infantry Officers' course at Number Six Officer Cadet Battalion in Oxford, beginning 1 December and concluding in March 1917.

The news seems to have come to Will like a bolt from the skies. Suddenly, his world had changed again.

When the reality sank in, he must have felt very pleased. To top off the privilege of being selected, he was to study at Oxford, one of the oldest and most prestigious universities in the world. Of course the cadets would not be considered actual students of the University, but still, the phrase 'studying at Oxford' had a pleasant ring to it.

His exhilaration at the prospect might have been tempered, however, by a wistful regret. His comrades of the 39th would go into battle without him.

The men with whom he had shared jokes and conviviality, hard work and the privations of hellish route marches; the men he had perhaps grown to view almost as brothers—they would be heading for the mud and blood of the trenches, while he enjoyed the dignified comforts of boarding at an English college.

Will must have longed to send his parents a cable straight away, telling them the good news. Knowing they would be conjecturing and fretting about his going to fight in some unknown country at any day, he would not want to waste a moment before setting their hearts at ease. Nonetheless, he was forced to wait. He and the other NCOs destined for the course were not released from camp until 25 November, when they caught the early train from Amesbury to London—two days after the 39th had departed.

The sky was overcast and a strong wind was blowing. As soon as Sergeant Palstra arrived in the capital he popped in to a shop and purchased a bottle of Eau de Cologne as a gift for his mother. Perfume was an expensive luxury she would never dream of buying for herself. Next he headed for the nearest post office and sent a cable to his parents announcing the good news, followed by the bottle of Eau de Cologne well wrapped in cardboard and brown paper.

Afterwards he and his fellow cadets splashed their way through the busy, wet streets to Paddington Station. There they boarded another train which took them fifty-five miles northwest alongside the Thames River, through the gently rolling green hills of South West England, towards Oxford. As the train steamed its way out of the city and into the English countryside the rain began to ease. Eventually the grey clouds broke apart and pale November sunshine streamed from the skies, dappling acres of wet meadows and leafless hedgerows, glimmering off fast-flowing streams.

Back in January 1915 a School of Instruction for young officers had been set up in Oxford. By March 1916 about three thousand officers had passed through the School. That same year, the School was superseded by two Officer Cadet Battalions formed at Oxford. These were No. 4 Oxford and No. 6 Balliol College. In these battalions, candidates for commissions, many of whom had served in the ranks, underwent a complete course of training for up to seven months.

The strength of each cadet battalion was about 750 men and they were housed by companies in Keble, Wadham, Hertford, New, Magdalen, Trinity, Balliol, St John's and Worcester Colleges[120]. Jesus College served as a Garrison Battalion. Will's company was to be quartered in Balliol.

During the Great War, Balliol had two distinct populations. Some of the older Fellows, along with a much-reduced student body, carried on something of the ordinary academic life of the college. But Balliol's premises, like those of most Oxford colleges, were largely given over to war work. Balliol hosted thousands of British and Commonwealth officer cadets on short training courses.

---

120   Oxford University Archives

These men were neither members of Balliol nor of the University of Oxford, but to Will this would hardly have mattered. The chance to study within such exalted halls was the opportunity—literally—of a lifetime.

The nineteenth century poet Mathew Arnold had deemed Oxford 'The City of Dreaming Spires';

'And that sweet city with her dreaming spires,
She needs not June for beauty's heightening.'

Indeed, Oxford needed nothing for beauty's heightening in the early winter of 1916. The pavements of the grand old city were trodden by dons in flapping black gowns, wielding walking sticks, and by striding soldiers in jodhpurs, and women in long skirts and straw hats, leading children by the hand. The city's cobbled roads carried cyclists and plodding cart-horses, and the occasional motor-car; her rivers and gleaming canals were thoroughfares for ducks and barges and sometimes—though not as often during wintry wartime—rowboats. Oxford's ornate buildings in the Gothic Revival style, delicate yet at the same time powerful and majestic, mingled with examples of every British architectural period since the arrival of the Saxons. Balliol College, within its spacious, parklike grounds, was impressive. Its main front was a Gothic range known as the Brackenbury Buildings, on Broad Street. As the Australian cadet officers passed through the main entrance beneath the central gate tower, they must have gazed up at the grand nineteenth century façade.

To some, this building looked like a hotel; to others it resembled a railway station. Perhaps in Will's eyes the Brackenbury Buildings seemed the gateway to a new life of which he'd scarcely dared to dream.

A RARE GLIMPSE OF WILL RELAXING IN A DECKCHAIR, CIRCA 1917.

Surrounded by reputed hauntings from the Middle Ages, serene gardens, soaring vaults and grotesque gothic fantasies in stone, Sergeant Palstra and his fellow officer cadets commenced their studies as the last leaves of autumn rained down on the university's lawns.

From January 1915 to February 1916, eleven groups of subalterns, five hundred men in all, passed through Balliol College on short training courses. The subalterns were followed by officer cadets: ten companies of a couple of hundred each, one after the other, between March 1916 and December 1918. The college assumed the character of a barracks, and the Garden Quad became a drill square. The few remaining dons might easily have resented this military takeover but they saw it as the College's contribution to the war effort and welcomed the cadets, taking an active interest in their work and amusements.[121]

The course consisted of Infantry Training 1914, in addition to training in leadership, tactics, weapons, military law, military accounting systems and military history. It was designed to test the cadets physically and mentally, and graduation was by no means guaranteed. Upon graduating, cadets would be promoted to the rank of second lieutenant.[122]

Sergeant Palstra and the other cadets were always on the alert for news concerning their comrades in France. On 2 December, the 39th marched into the war-broken city of Armentieres. There they became the battalion in support of the units holding the front line. They were close to the front, well within earshot of the booming guns, and for the first time they saw evidence of the havoc and destruction of war.

'The greater part of the population had deserted the city, except a few people who still lived in the houses, and gained a livelihood by keeping small cafes and postcard shops,' Captain Paterson would write later. 'The great weaving factories were all closed, but a few breweries still carried on their business.

---

121 John Jones, *Balliol College: a history* (Oxford University Press, 1997).

122 'Wapedia - Wiki: Royal Military College, Duntroon', http://wapedia.mobi/en/Royal_Military_College_Duntroon. 'Second lieutenant' is a junior commissioned officer military rank

'This part of the front was quiet. The city itself was shelled, and the people who lived in it had become familiar with bursting shells and poison gas. War to a great extent had lost its terrors for them, and they went about their daily business with a strange fatalistic shrug of the shoulders and with the murmured 'C'est la guerre'[123] which greeted each misfortune or trial.'

'Three days later the battalion received its first casualty when a private was wounded by a shell splinter. The following day the 39th lost its first officer when Lieutenant Basil White, in charge of a working party making essential repairs in the trenches, died of wounds received through the premature explosion of a Newton Pippin rifle grenade.'

At this news a sombre mood settled on the 39th. That a young lieutenant had lost his life after only four days at the front was a depressing thought. After that training, all that hope, his life had been snuffed out. White had been very popular with all the men. They felt sorry, too, for his parents.

Receiving this news in Oxford, how did Will feel? His usual mood seems to have been one of quiet equanimity. The strong faith on which he had been reared sustained him. He knew without doubt that White had gone to heaven and that some day everyone would meet again there. Furthermore, if we read between the lines we might conclude that, like many young men, he felt utterly certain that God had intended him for great things; and that therefore he would survive. Perhaps this certainty buoyed him, driving his desire to achieve yet loftier heights.

More reports trickled in from France. Paterson reported that, 'On 9 December the 39th relieved the 37th on the front line. . . The men of the battalion found themselves facing the enemy lines with only the narrow, mysterious strip of No Man's Land between themselves and the Hun.'[124]

The 39th Battalion was receiving its 'baptism of fire'.

---

123   C'est la guerre – That's war.

124   Paterson

The English mail continued to take a long time to get through to Australia, and even telegrams were being held up. Not only war, but the vagaries of the telegraphic system were probably to blame. The submarine cables of the Telegraph Construction and Maintenance Company, lying along the seabeds between Australia and Europe, were subject to the whims of current, tide and reef. Faults were common.

By 11 December, sixteen days after it was sent, Will's telegram still had not reached his parents. It was only now that they were receiving correspondence he had posted weeks earlier, while training on Salisbury Plain. Believing that the 39th must surely have departed for active combat—probably to France—taking their son with it, Wiebe and Jacoba turned to their faith to ease their burden of worry. All they could do was pray, hope for the best, and continue to send letters and parcels.

On that day Will's mother sat down and wrote him a letter. She had placed it in an envelope ready to be posted, when Will's father arrived home with a telegram in his hands. At the sight of that dreaded paper, her heart raced. In her own words:

> My dear Will,
>
> This letter was closed and ready to be posted, when Dad came home at lunch time with your cable. I felt my heart beating when I saw him, but something in his face reassured me, when he called me to the front room, and my word what good news!!
>
> We cried and we laughed and congratulated one another, so glad we were for your sake. My word this will bring good cheer on Xmas to us, our hearty congratulations. I have not seen Dad so excited for a long, long time. Just fancy you going to Balliol College Oxford, he feels that his boys are doing A1. Now we are anxious to know how it all came about, if it is still a result of you applying for the Flying Corps or if you went up for an exam. What ever

it is I am awfully pleased and it was only nine months after you entered camp. Well done I am sure! Of course Dad was glad for my sake as he carefully explained, but how he tried he could not hide, he was as proud as punch.

The next thing was that nobody was to talk about it, before it was all 'bevestigd',[125] but I can't see how he can keep it to himself, he is simply full of it. Frank was of course 'perverse' and said, 'I'll skite about my brother as much as I like'. I did not tell him, but gave him the cable and it was just as though a ray of sunshine struck him from head to foot. He was pleased. Vic of course feels himself more important from day to day on account of his brothers. I must say they all felt mightily happy about it.

Once more, many congratulations and a hearty kiss,

from your loving

mother.

Throughout that exceptionally cold winter, Will and his fellow officer cadets trained at Oxford, while overseas the Great War raged on.

Will was indeed fortunate to have been in Oxford during the first few months the rest of the Third Division was in France. Across the channel in Flanders the 1916-1817 winter was the most rigorous in the memory of the Flemish peasants, and Australian troops suffered greatly. They were not used to all that snow and ice, not to mention the mud. In the trenches of France the cold seemed to penetrate to the very marrow of the men's bones.

In January, 1917, General Monash wrote to his wife from France, 'About a week ago it snowed heavily and then it froze, and for the last six days the day temperature has stood at 2 degrees below freezing, and the night temperature at 17 degrees below freezing. Can you realise what this means? The whole country is frozen hard, and there is not a drop of

---

125   Bevestigd: A Dutch word meaning 'confirmed'.

water to be had. The ground is frozen hard three feet deep, and what was mud a week ago is now solid rock. All drains, ponds, ditches, and streams are solid masses of ice. Everybody is skating on all canals and rivers.'

Burton wrote, 'Snow had an unfortunate capacity for sopping through boots, and cold feet were almost the limit of torture. Cold wood and cold iron seemed almost to burn in blue and bloodless hands. Shaving when the ice was almost forming on the tin of water was a butcherly performance. Men wrapped themselves up in all the clothes they could possibly lay hands upon: balaclavas, scarves, extra underwear, leather waistcoats, gloves, extra socks, sandbags, overcoats; they sealed up dugouts as hermetically as possible; they salvaged benzine tins and made braziers and burnt therein all that came to hand in the way of fuel. Still, they shivered.'[126]

The men on active service wore cardigan jackets, fur and leather jerkins and great-coats, and this additional clothing, with fighting equipment buckled on over it, made it difficult at times for two men to pass each other in a trench. Coke fires in braziers provided a little warmth, but lights had to be used with utmost caution.[127]

What of Charles Palstra? Having received his commission, he had left Australia on 20 November with reinforcements for the 46th. He was now back with his own battalion, on Salisbury Plain.

Despite the fact that they were separated by many miles, the brothers managed to catch up with each other when their leaves coincided.

On Sunday 11 February Charles boarded the train from Salisbury and Will caught the train from Oxford. The brothers rendezvoused in the crowded tea-rooms of London's Waterloo station. Imagine them grinning from ear to ear they shook hands vigorously and eyed each other from head to foot. Both were clad in khaki, with British-style caps on

---

126   Burton, 'Chapter XVIII, The Silent Division: New Zealanders at the Front, 1914-1919'.

127   Paterson

their heads. Will sported his sergeant's stripes, and Charles—the taller of the two—his company sergeant major's insignia in addition to his Provost Marshal's badge. No doubt each complimented the other on their rise through military ranks.

The brothers spent half an hour together catching up on news, before the train to Warwick pulled in at the platform and Will had to board it. In that historic town, he and the other cadet officers were about to undertake a week-long musketry course. The brothers parted in a cloud of smoke and steam as the train pulled slowly away from the platform, no doubt wishing each other 'good luck' and 'God speed'.

On 12 February, Will wrote to his parents to allay their worries telling them he had met with his brother Charles in England, and that he was looking fit and well. He mentioned that just before he had left Oxford, his Christmas parcel had arrived at last, full of knitted garments from his mother and good things to eat! Tactfully, he omitted from his correspondence the fact that his initial excitement at being chosen for the Infantry Officers' course had lately been giving way to some disillusionment. The course, he admitted later in his 'War Experiences', was not of as high a standard as it should have been. Indeed, in some areas it was sadly lacking—in weapons training, for example. So far the cadets had practised with no other weapons than rifles, and it looked as if training at Warwick would be no different.

Typically understating any criticism, Will would write,

> In the meantime, as a reward for three months of strenuous work as Brigade Orderly Room Sergeant, I was selected to do a four months course at an Officer Cadet Battalion, Oxford. Looking back on my period there I feel that the training might have been a little more practical with advantage.

It was not Will's way, however, to challenge the authorities. He had been brought up to respect those who were in charge, and he submitted to whatever was asked of him without complaint.

By the close of February some two hundred men, a quarter of them either Anzacs or Canadians, had enjoyed four months' temporary membership of Balliol. After a rousing celebratory farewell dinner on the last weekend in March, the final War Office Exam was held at Worcester College. The results were published the following day.

In his diary, Will wrote:

'Wedn. 28th March. Results—5th in Coy 80%. Commissioned A.I.F. List 189.'

This terse, bland sentence concealed all the triumph and exultation of success. That he, an erstwhile accountant with no tertiary education, should come fifth out of all the cadets in the company was a tremendous boost to his self-confidence.

He had received the coveted commission! It was only thirteen months since he had first boarded the train for the Ballarat Training Camp as a lowly private, but that seemed a lifetime ago. He must have felt different in every respect; far more confident, physically stronger, and imbued with a sense of destiny and a feeling that the sky—literally—was the limit. He had been measured against his peers and counted among the elite. If he could achieve such success, he was certainly capable of becoming an aviator—for that remained his premier ambition, and his determination to fly grew stronger as time went by.

Second Lieutenant Palstra

Will now held the rank of Second Lieutenant. As soon as had had a spare moment he cabled his parents with the good news.

All those who had passed the examination were immediately issued with their officers' stars and belt. From that moment, the attitude of every drill sergeant who had ever harangued them changed utterly. NCOs stood to attention and saluted, calling the graduates 'sir'.

Officers grinned and shook them by the hand, welcoming them as equals. It was a grand feeling!

On Tuesday 17 April 1917 George V, King of England, once again reviewed the Australian and New Zealand troops at Bulford Field on Salisbury Plain. That was a momentous day in more ways than one.

On Second Lieutenant Palstra's return from the march, tired but triumphant, his ears still ringing with the music of the brass bands, his mind still filled with the vision of thousands of men in smart uniforms and horses in shining accoutrements, he was handed his orders for France.

This must have brought him down to earth with a jolt.

There could be no delay. Straight away, he and two of his fellow freshly-graduated fellow officers—Second Lieutenants Ricketts and Speering—along with some platoons of reinforcements, packed their belongings and boarded the train to London. After arrival, Will sent a cable to his parents, as soon as he had a free moment to visit the post office.

He was on his way to the front line.

Oxford in 1917

Part X 1917: Across the Straits of Dover

1917: Across the Straits of Dover | 1: The Guns Thundered all Night Long

There's a township torn and shattered,

There are streets of broken brick

Where the shells have crumped and battered,

Where the mule teams rear and kick,

And the sweating driver curses

As the pellets zip and tear;

Oh confound this German shrapnel,

"Up, you blighters, c'est la guerre." [128]

By 1917 London's Victoria Station, a beautiful Edwardian baroque building, had been open for fifty-seven years. From its dim caverns a direct rail link ran to the main railway station on the coast in Folkestone, where the ferries embarked for France. During the Great

---

[128] --C. in New Zealand at the Front. From 'The Silent Division: New Zealanders at the Front, 1914-1919' by O E Burton. 1935.

War Victoria Station became a terminus for trains carrying soldiers to and from France, many of them wounded.

After sliding away from the busy platforms, Second Lieutenant Palstra's train navigated its way along the lines through London and out into the English countryside. Imagine Will, seated in an officers' compartment filled to capacity with other officers, gazing out the windows wrapped in thought, as the engine chugged across the miles, through the hop-fields of Kent towards the chalk cliffs of the coast.[129]

At the bustling port town of Folkestone on the English Channel, they detrained. From Folkestone on a clear day, the long, low outline of France would be visible across the Straits of Dover. On the day Will arrived, however, the weather was overcast and wet. Waiting at the dockside with his men, Will might well have turned up the collar of his greatcoat against the chilly slap of wind and rain.

Paddlewheel ferries ran from Folkestone's harbour to the ancient city of Boulogne on the other side of the channel. One of these vessels was waiting for Will and his men. They packed themselves among the crowds of other soldiers aboard the sharp-bowed cross-channeller, which soon cast off and headed into the rough, grey seas, full steam ahead. Before long the ship reached her full speed of twenty knots. Pitching and plunging on the choppy waves, destroyers edged in to escort the ship.

Numerous vessels dotted the waters of the English Channel – troopers, destroyers, patrol boats and cargo vessels.

Day and night the Channel transports conveyed their freight of men from the shores of England to the great army bases in France. Day and night, minesweeping fleets scoured the Straits of Dover, and the destroyer flotillas patrolled the Channel, from Ushant to the Nore, in order that the traffic of war might go on, unimpeded by the attacks of enemy submarines or the danger of floating mines.[130]

---

129   This visualisation is inspired by a description in G.D. Mitchell's 'Backs to the Wall.'

130   Colonel A T Paterson, 'The 39th'.

At length the paddle steamer docked in the Port of Boulogne.

When the rhythmic thudding of the ferry's engines ceased to fill Will's ears, sounds that were more ominous began to emerge from behind the pattering of the rain and the bluster of the wind. The men shouldered their belongings, and perhaps, as the commanding officer issued orders to them in a loud, clear voice, he glanced measuringly at each face. They must have heard and felt it too—the continuous thudding and rumbling, of low intensity but immense volume. All knew that for the duration of their stay in France, that dull thunder would wax and wane, never absent from their lives. They had even heard it in England at times, especially during a big assault.[131] It carried across fifty miles; the booming of the guns along the front.

Second Lieutenant William Palstra, along with the other commissioned officers, were directed to relatively comfortable lodgings at Boulogne's 'Hotel Louvre'. That evening Will wrote in his war diary with his typical succinct style: '18th London. Victoria—Folkestone. 7.30 pm Boulogne. Stayed Hotel Louvre.'

Reveille rang out across the camps early the following morning. Will and his fellow officers spent most of that day, 19 April 1917, in Boulogne with the reinforcements. The rain tapered off completely, and late that afternoon they shouldered their kit once more and assembled at the Gare Centrale, the Central Railway Station, ready to board a train to the town of Étaples.

At half past five the troop-trains pulled out of the Gare Centrale. They put the miles behind them with ponderous slowness, halting with exasperating regularity at intervals of

---

131   In his journal (Medicine and Duty), Canadian doctor Harold McGill mentions that when he arrived in Boulogne France for the first time, he could hear and feel 'a low-pitched continuous thudding and rumbling of low intensity but immense volume' — the sound of the guns, which he says was scarcely absent in the three years he spent in France. The guns could also be heard in England at times, especially during a big assault. Source: hmsvictory on Tumblr.com and http://4yearsofww1.info/ retrieved on 19th November 2015.

twenty minutes or so. Seated in the grimy carriages,[132] the men were quite content to watch the panorama of this new country slowly unfolding before their eyes, or to stroll along the line beside the barely-moving train.

Beneath clearing skies they passed through beautiful countryside, brushed by springtime. Startling white splashes of blossom bedecked the hedges, trees were enveloped in the green haze of new leaves, cool sunlight rinsed buildings of mellow stone. Church steeples peeped among the tiled roofs of villages, while fields lay pockmarked with shell-holes.

Paterson wrote of the men of the 39th, most of whom were seeing France for the first time, that some wished to demonstrate their knowledge of the country, and unhesitatingly pronounced every building which could boast a turret or tower to be a 'chateau', thus calling attention to many an unpretentious country house.[133]

C.E.W. Bean, writing of his arrival in France at the same time of year 12 months earlier, gives us an eloquent description of the sights Will and his companions would likely have seen[134]. Magnificent draught horses were working in the rich, brown fields. The figures that drove the harrows were usually that of an old man or a young boy; or, once or twice, of a woman.

Women were digging in the fields everywhere, or trudging home along the roads, bent beneath great bundles of firewood. The country was almost all cultivated land, one vast farming industry, and they had managed to get through the whole year's work exactly as if the men were there. As far as the eye could see every field was ploughed, every green crop springing. On observing this CW Bean wrote, 'I think it a wonderful performance.[135]'

The main thoroughfares were crowded with military vehicles. At every country cross-road where there was likely to be a congestion of the great lumbering motor-lorries a British

---

132   Somme Mud

133   Source: Paterson

134   'Letters From France' by CEW Bean.

135   C E W Bean 'Letters From France'

policeman could be seen directing the traffic. Other policemen were standing outside ruined village churches which the long-range guns had knocked to pieces in trying to get at a supply dump or a headquarters, or on point duty at the ruined farmhouses which it was unhealthy at certain hours of the day to pass. These watchmen were keeping a very close and critical eye upon all passers-by.

Will's train finally pulled into Étaples at half past six, with the passengers [136] no doubt complaining about the slowness of the trip.

The platoons of reinforcements were thus directed by the big hand of General Headquarters, marching out of the station and along the streets that led out of town, to the sprawling acreage of tents where the enlisted men (and presumably the NCOs) would temporarily be housed. Swamped with sand and surrounded by mud flats, this large and complex tent city encircled the town.

161 Westgarth Str.,

Northcote, 20-4-17

My dear Will,

So at last it has come, the news came through yesterday—you have gone over to France. I knew after we received your cable about your promotion, that I could expect it every moment. Perhaps it is because I have been thinking about it such a lot, that now it came in reality I could take it with great calmness. You know you have spoiled us a great deal, one with your cheerfulness and the other with always making the best of the circumstances.

It is not a small thing to see your sons go off on such a dangerous mission as this war calls our boys to. So when we saw you off last year about this time we felt as though the light was fading out of our lives and that only God

---

136   Will wrote rather sarcastically in his diary: '19th Left Gare Centrale 5.30 pm. Arrived Étaples 6.30 pm — 18 miles. Good going!?'

knew what darkness we had to face. And a year has passed and as well with Charlie as with you there have been so many unexpected cheerful tidings, that I cannot do otherwise than thank the Lord. And now I must pray more fervently than ever for you and trust Him more fully than ever. He is mighty to keep, and if it is His will, He will do so.

Of course the whole family felt it very much the moment the news came to us, and then of course our different minds started to work, we knew as much that you were going as 2nd Lieutenant but where did you belong to? Your training had been more on Staff work at H.Q. and lectures, where were they going to use you for, there was great scope for discussion and every one of them alarmed that they had the right look on the matter.

The girls sent you back to your old place at H.Q. and as this did not clash with my wishes, I agreed. I know that the first chance you will have, you'll write us all about it—but what a time before it reaches us! Still it would be mean to complain, I am so thankful you send us these cables they make me feel like this—I am longing for letters but—I know the latest! There is not so much room for unduly doubt and fear.

You did not mention Charlie, that means he is still on the plains, mails are coming in so irregular and with weeks between, I expect the next one several at the time, but till up now I do not know more about him since his arrival then that he attends a machine gun school. He is a splendid writer but his letters lack sometimes plain information, I suppose he forgets to put it in…

On the same day that Jacoba was writing this letter in Melbourne, Second Lieutenant Palstra awoke to his first morning in Étaples with the long, low rumble of distant guns in his ears. Occasionally this might have been punctuated by dull 'pops' of shrapnel bursting among the clouds, as British ant-aircraft guns opened fire on German aeroplanes. Will and his fellow subalterns were billeted in the home of one of the citizens, who had opened their homes to the war effort, billeting soldiers by the hundred.

On the 22nd April 1917, the night before he led his column of reinforcements to the battle front, Will Palstra prayed. He prayed every night of his life, but on this particular occasion these are, perhaps, close to the words he said – the soldier's prayer:

> Almighty and Everlasting God, by whose Grace Thy servants are enabled to fight the good fight of faith and ever prove victorious. We humbly beseech Thee so to inspire us, that we may yield our hearts to thine obedience and, exercise our wills on Thy behalf. Help us to think wisely: to speak rightly: to resolve bravely: to act kindly: to live purely. Bless us in body and in soul, and make us a blessing to our comrades. Whether at home or abroad may we ever seek the extension of Thy Kingdom. Let the assurance of Thy presence save us from sinning: support us in life, and comfort us in death. O Lord our God accept this prayer for Jesus Christ's sake. Amen.[137]

While not so very far away on the Western Front, the guns thundered all night long.

---

137 WW1 Soldiers' prayer, from a leaflet pasted inside the bible of Private Frank Lankshear, 7140, 6th Squadron., Royal Flying Corps and, Royal Army Ordnance Corps who died of wounds received in aerial combat at the age of 22 on Tuesday 21 August 1917.

If you have enjoyed this book, please review it on Amazon or Goodreads.

Goodreads: https://www.goodreads.com/

Amazon USA: https://www.amazon.com/

Amazon UK: https://www.amazon.co.uk/

Amazon Australia: https://www.amazon.com.au/

For information about Leaves of Gold Press books—past, present and forthcoming—read our newsletter.

https://www.leavesofgoldpress.com/home-2/subscribe/

Visit the Airship of Dreams channel on YouTube @AirshipofDreams and the Leaves of Gold Press channel, @LeavesofGoldPress

BIBLIOGRAPHY

The Australian Imperial Force (AIF)

Books:

- Bean, C.E.W. *Letters from France.* London: Cassell, 1917.

- Carlyon, Les. *The Great War.* Pan Macmillan Australia, 2007.

- Davies, Will. *In the Footsteps of Private Lynch.* Vintage Books, Random House, 2008.

- Dunne, Barry. *The 39th.* Accessed September 7, 2023. http://sites.google.com/site/the39th/.

- Green, Frank C. *The Fortieth: A Record of the 40th Battalion* A.I.F. Govt. Printer, Hobart, Tasmania, Australia.

- Hunter, Doug. *Voyages to War: the AIF at Sea.*

- Lewis, Brian. *Our War: A View of World War 1 From Inside an Australian Family.* Penguin Books, 1980.

- Lynch, E.P.F. *Somme Mud.* Originally published 1921. New edition, Random House, 2006.

- Matthews, Wayne, and David Wilson. *Fighting Nineteenth: History of the 19th Infantry Battalion AIF* 1915-1918. Australian Military History Publications, 2011.

- Mitchell, G.D. *Backs to the Wall: A Larrikin on the Western Front.* Angus & Robertson, 89 Castlereagh St., Sydney, 1937.

- Paterson, A.T. *The Thirty-ninth: the history of the 39th Battalion, Australian Imperial Force.* G.W. Green & Sons, Melbourne, 1934.

- Pedersen, Peter, with Chris Roberts. *Anzacs on the Western Front: The Australian War Memorial Battlefield Guide.* Wiley, 2012.

- Thomas, Helen. *As it Was and World Without End.* London: William Heinemann, 1931.

- Travers, Richard C. *Diggers in France: Australian Soldiers on the Western Front.* ABC Books, 2008.

- Wills, Gabriele. *The Great War as You May Not Know it. Odd, Intriguing and Surprising Facts about WW1.* Accessed September 7, 2023. http://4yearsofww1.info.

- Wolff, Leon. *In Flanders Fields: the 1917 Campaign.* The Folio Society London, 2003.

Primary Sources:

- Australian War Memorial Histories. *Australian Imperial Force unit war diaries, 1914-18 War - AWM4 Subclass 23/10 - 10th Infantry Brigade.* Accessed September 7, 2023. www.awm.gov.au/collection/C1343669.

- Australian War Memorial Histories. *Australian Imperial Force unit war diaries, 1914-18 War. Official War Diaries of the 10th Brigade June 1917.* AWM4 23/10/8 - June 1917.

- Australian War Memorial Histories. *Chapter XV – The Battle of Messines – June 7th.* PDF file, 2.5Mb.

- Australian War Memorial Histories. *War diaries 39th Battalion AIF.* Accessed September 7, 2023. (online source).

- Carthew, Noel. *Voices from the Trenches; Letters to Home.* New Holland, 2002.

- McKinlay, William Ernest. *Ways and By-Ways of a Singing Kiwi With The N.Z. Divisional Entertainers in France. 1939.* Accessed September 7, 2023. (online source).

- Williams, No. 538 Cpl. Ivor Alexander. *Diary of My Trip Abroad 1915-19. 21st Battalion Australian Imperial Forces.*

The Salvation Army in the First World War
Books:

- Bond, Lieut. Colonel. *The Army That Went With the Boys: A Record of Salvation Army Work with the AIF.* Salvation Army Printing Office, East Melbourne, 1919.

- Bradwell, Cyril R. *Fight the Good Fight: The Story of The Salvation Army in New Zealand 1883-1983.* Reed, 1982.

AIRSHIP OF DREAMS

The Doomed Flight of the Titanic of the Skies

VALIANT HEART 1

"Airship of Dreams" is a true story. It stands alone and can be read by itself, although it is also Book #1 of the VALIANT HEART trilogy. The book tells William Palstra's extraordinary life story; a life that ended in 1930 when His Majesty's airship R101 exploded catastrophically, changing the world forever.

An Air Force pilot and decorated hero, Palstra returns to Australia in 1919, at the end of the First World War. We follow his marriage and family, his role in the expansion of Melbourne University, and his rise through the ranks of the newly-formed Royal Australian Airforce (RAAF).

The decade of the 1920s was the Golden Age of Airships and zeppelins. The stuff of dreams, these enormous, cigar-shaped aircraft glided slowly and majestically across the skies, like fantastic creatures from legend.

The British Empire's R101 was the world's biggest airship at that time. She was fitted out so luxuriously that she has been called The Titanic of the Skies. And like the Titanic, her maiden voyage was doomed.

"Airship of Dreams" tells of this fatal flight, and the repercussions of the tragedy that rippled through time and continues to exert its influence to this very day.

Valiant Heart Trilogy

Book 1: Airship of Dreams
Book 2: The Call to Arms
Book 3: Blood and Fire

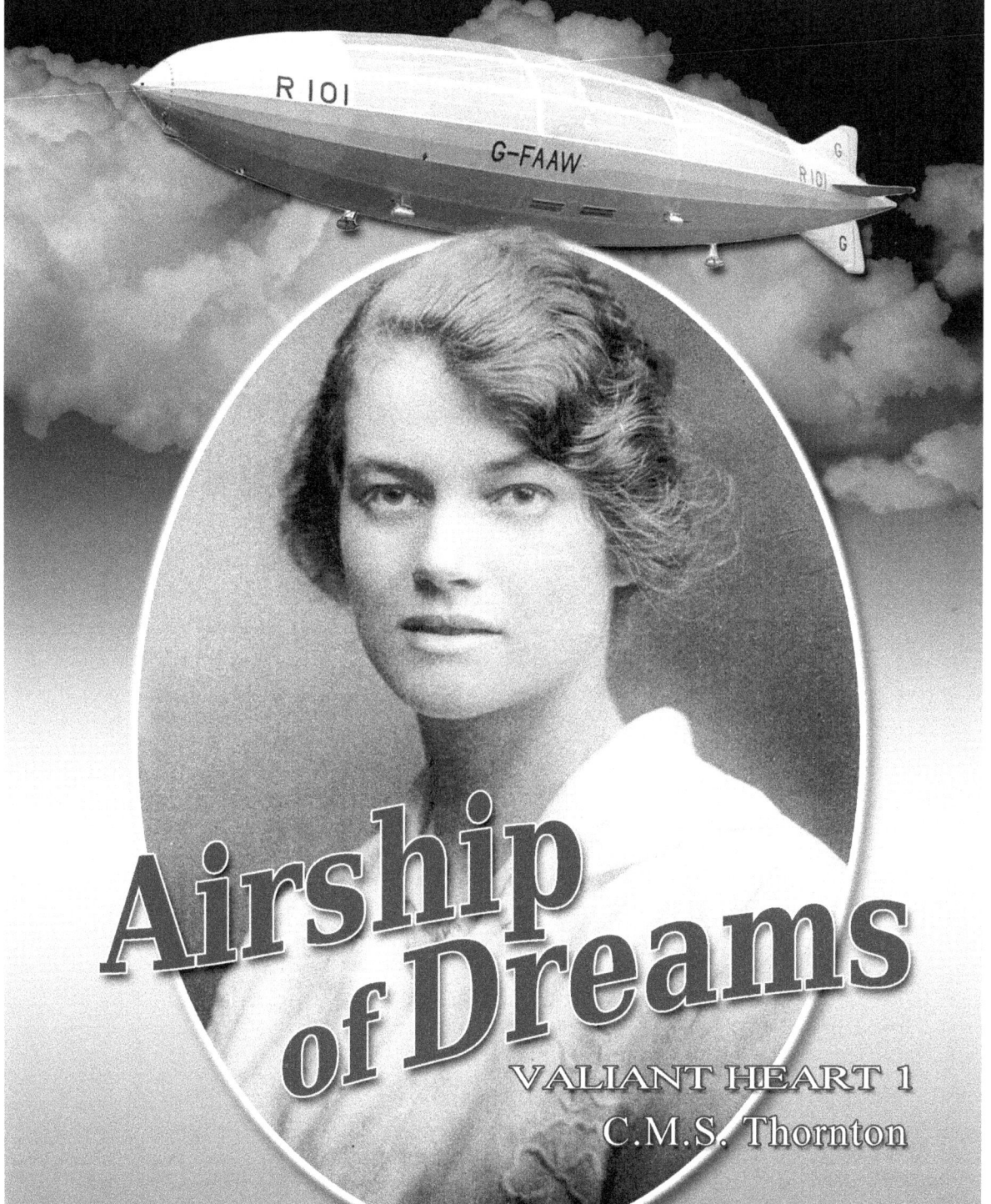

Airship of Dreams

VALIANT HEART 1
C.M.S. Thornton

The Doomed Flight of the Titanic of the Skies

BLOOD AND FIRE

The Hero Who Conquered the Skies

VALIANT HEART 3

This is the story of First World War hero William Palstra between 1917 and 1919. Fighting the trenches on the Western Front with the 39th Battalion AIF, the Battle of Messines, being awarded a Military Cross by the King at Buckingham Palace, joining the Australian Flying Corps and learning to fly biplanes, braving artillery fire and enemy planes while flying over enemy lines, Armistice Day 1918 and the celebrations in Paris, the happy and victorious homecoming.

"Blood and Fire" is Book #3 of the VALIANT HEART trilogy following Palstra's story as he walks through the valley of death and emerges a hero.

Valiant Heart Trilogy

Book 1: Airship of Dreams
Book 2: The Call to Arms
Book 3: Blood and Fire

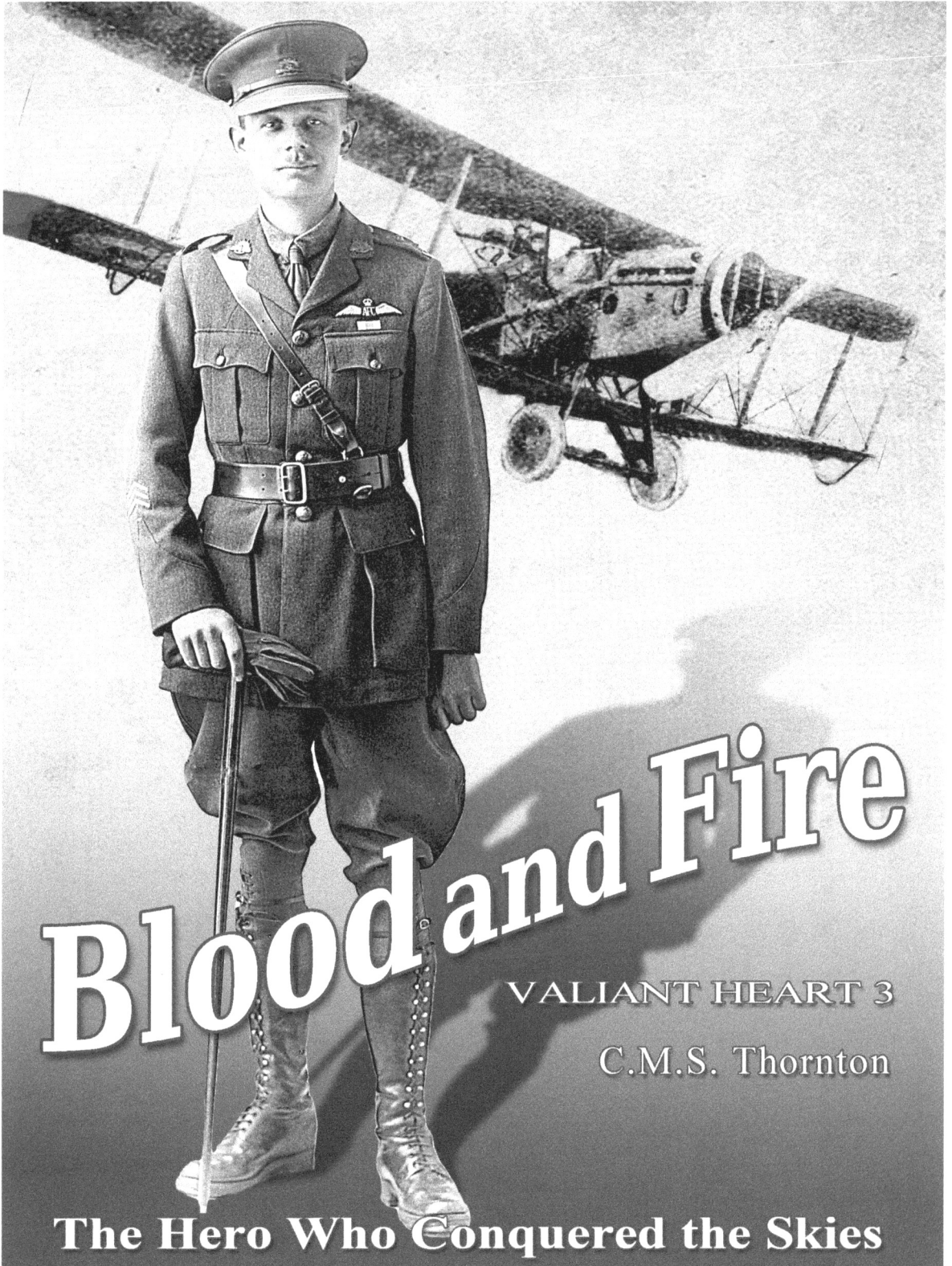

The Call to Arms

www.ingramcontent.com/pod-product-compliance
Lightning Source LLC
Chambersburg PA
CBHW041238240426
43661CB00070B/2916